RICHARD COOKE

TIRED OF WINNING

A

CHRONICLE

OF

AMERICAN

DECLINE

Black Inc.

Published by Black Inc.,
an imprint of Schwartz Publishing Pty Ltd
Level 1, 221 Drummond Street Carlton VIC 3053, Australia
enquiries@blackincbooks.com www.blackincbooks.com

Copyright © Richard Cooke 2019
Richard Cooke asserts his right to be known as the author of this work.

ALL RIGHTS RESERVED.
No part of this publication may be reproduced, stored in a retrieval system, or
transmitted in any form by any means electronic, mechanical, photocopying,
recording or otherwise without the prior consent of the publishers.

Quotations in this book appear as in the original sources,
including any spelling or grammatical errors.

9781760641146 (paperback)
9781743820834 (ebook)

 A catalogue record for this
book is available from the
National Library of Australia

Cover design by Akiko Chan
Cover image © Getty Images
Text design by Tristan Main
Typesetting by Marilyn de Castro

To Loulou

CONTENTS

We're going to win so much. You're going to get tired of winning, you're going to say, 'Please, Mr President, I have a headache. Please, don't win so much. This is getting terrible.'

Donald Trump, South Carolina (2016)

… And Pedlar Forrest shot Jim Gym.
And Jim Gym shot James McBride.
And James McBride shot Cyrus Partovi.
And Cyrus Partovi shot Lewis P. Bohler.
And James Earl Ray shot Martin Luther King …

J.G. Ballard, 'The Generations of America' (1968)

AUTHOR'S NOTE

The impulse to write this book began with a failure. I visited the United States before, during and after the 2016 presidential election campaign and did not understand what I saw. After leaving the country, this feeling nagged at me until I returned, eighteen months later, in the lead-up to the 2018 midterm elections. This time, I was determined to experience as much of the present state of the United States as I could, and to capture that experience on behalf of those similarly perplexed.

I felt there was more than enough reporting on the US president without adding to it. The harried ranks of foreign correspondents were thinning, and the survivors sometimes seemed trapped in New York City and Washington, D.C., as though permanently assigned to the president's Twitter feed. Meanwhile, the relayed images of the United States beyond this unpromising horizon were becoming lower and lower in resolution. Midterms are given less weighting than contests for the White House, but they are seldom less consequential, and the 2018 ballot was the most important in a generation. It was a referendum on

Trumpism rather than on Trump, and its diffuse and fragmentary nature meant a book could be written around it, rather than about it, and across a wider landscape than a few battleground states.

The question 'what is the United States like today?' also turned out to be of domestic interest. It is not rare for metropolitan Americans to visit the heartland or the South, but it is not common either, and the coast-dwellers were the people most curious to ask me about what it was 'like'. The tone of these discussions was not hopeful ('So are we fucked?' was a standard enquiry after a couple of drinks) and one eminent historian asked me, not as an exercise, if I thought there would be a second Civil War soon. I said I didn't know, and twenty states later I still don't.

'Decline' is a laden word, especially in the subtitle of a book, and it's possible that Gibbon and Spengler have given it a permanent taint of melodrama. But I can think of no other way to describe the conditions I encountered. That decline may be temporary, relative, aberrational or partial, but it is real. In some places it made me despondent; elsewhere, resilience and rebirth leavened my pessimism.

One indicative episode: near mission's end, I was in Arcadia, California, and on a single day found myself within driving distance of both the site of a mass shooting and the front of an unprecedented forest blaze. I did not get in the car: I had met my grim quota of these acts of god and man many months earlier. When I read reports of the shooting – some of the dead had survived a previous spree killing in Las Vegas – the targeted advertising on my computer offered up a bullet-resistant children's backpack. That object should not exist.

I am not sure what to call the dispatches that make up this book. Other languages have more nuanced and adaptive names for hybrids of reportage and essay, writing that modulates between reporting and reflection, but in English we are stuck with catch-alls: accounts, reports, missives. At least two of my countryfolk – Robert Hughes and Maria Tumarkin – have combined thematically linked essays into mosaic pictures, and this approach suits topics that are too expansive for a unitary theory. My own subject, America in the twenty-first century, is also on this scale.

So what business is it of mine? Being an outsider has its advantages, and there is a long tradition of interlopers shrewdly chronicling America, dating all the way back to Alexis de Tocqueville. My nationality helped my cause as well: I was familiar – my country shares a cultural affinity with the United States – but not familiar enough to breed contempt. As an Australian, I was seldom received as a representative of the media elite, and there were times when natural selection broadened my accent into Crocodile Hunter territory. I should also mention, though it is distasteful, that white privilege has its uses. Even spatially it functioned as an access-all-areas pass, and it accounts for some of the things people were willing to say to me out loud.

I did not set out to assemble a prosecutorial brief, or to indict a nation and its citizens. Instead I took my bearings from history – in particular, I thought of the symmetry offered by the year 1968. That season of tumult, violence and change in the United States makes the present look survivable, if not surmountable. But when I met witnesses to this time, they invariably said things were worse now than they were fifty years ago. This might be recency bias – it's difficult to recall the pain of unfresh wounds – but I think there is a special, twice-bitten form of distress in the current scenario, in its abandoned promises, unrealised dreams and misappropriated resources. In the 1990s, John Berger could write that the poverty of the twentieth century was unlike that of any other time, because 'it is not, as poverty was before, the result of natural scarcity, but of a set of priorities imposed upon the rest of the world by the rich'. In the twenty-first century, the abyss between what could be and what is has extended further still.

It is true that America was never great for Americans of colour (or others who found themselves subject to its sadisms) and that the 'Make America Great Again' phenomenon is only a new version of an old nativist tendency, rather than some novelty emerging from the ether. But I think any cold comfort offered by familiarity is chilled further by an abiding sense of failure. More than fifty years on, the aims of the Civil Rights Act and the Great Society – the elimination of poverty and racial injustice – are so far from realisation that these policies could almost be begun afresh. African-American men are worse off economically than they were in the 1960s, and the energetic achievement of the first black presidency has been marred by an equal and opposite reaction.

Since the election of Trump, political science has tried to establish whether it is economic anxiety or racial animus that fuels his supporters. At first the answer seems obvious: when Trump warmed up his presidential run with the fraudulent accusation that Barack Obama was an African called 'Barry Soweto', it was not a tactic aimed at the hearts of the financially precarious. But the complex reality is that economic anxiety expresses itself through racial animus, and both find synergy in the punitive demonstrations of what is effectively an economic caste system. Perhaps most disturbingly, this social framework often requires no malice or even significant agency to operate (part of the reason why accusations of racism are received with such defensiveness).

When the South switched its vote from Democratic to Republican after the passing of the Civil Rights Act, it proved that racial segregation was not merely important to many of its citizens, but more important than *every other issue combined.* It was a principle so sacred that the South chose to raze institutions rather than desegregate them. In Arkansas in 1958, the state closed every public high school for twelve months. Legally desegregated funfairs all over the South simply closed, and in Lynchburg, Virginia, oddly shaped parks still carry the outline of paved-over public pools that lost their status as 'whites only'.

In cheerless moments, the principles impelling the Trump presidency feel like a relative of this drive, a project to destroy the United States rather than share its bounty across the colour bar. A lazy, loudmouth and easily distracted chief executive does not even seem a very efficient vector for this, and the rising tranche of right-wing politicians bathing in his light will be of greater concern. Yet opposition to them is already energised and enraged, as I discovered, and these coming generations will fight tenaciously for the United States of the future – if in the future it can still carry that name.

There will also be conflict in another space, one I feel compelled to mention. When I was writing these pieces, I often had the disorientating sensation of being in two countries at once: the United States, and the internet of the United States, which felt like a separate and sometimes more real entity than the corporeal locales. The effects of this are so various that they would take a book, or many books, to describe fully. (One small observation: it is noticeably harder to strike up conversation with a stranger without the mediation of a screen.) I have not written that book – instead, this online nation is a sub-theme that now and then gets closer attention, as in 'Notes on Some Artefacts'.

'Reality has a way of being not so external after all,' wrote John Steinbeck in his own chronicle of America. But I did not go on an exploration, seeking inner enlightenment. It would be bogus to hold back my thoughts and feelings on what I witnessed, but wherever possible I have put the words and thoughts of other people first. It is their lives, and their nation, that I have tried to reflect. And it is these Americans who have ultimately turned my ambivalence into a hesitant hope.

Richard Cooke
Hangzhou, China, 2019

TESTING TIMES

When a physician suspects something is wrong with a patient's sense of reality, she may ask them a question: 'Who is the president of the United States?' This is part of a protocol called the Mental Status Examination and evaluates a quality named orientation – the ability to discern the here and now. Since the elevation of Donald Trump to the White House, this simple test has lost some of its diagnostic precision. One Emergency doctor, Jeremy Samuel Faust, told *Slate* that 'regardless of political affiliation, my patients' reactions have shown that they find the truth to be far stranger – and more surprising – than fiction'.

This chronic sensation of unreality extends past the wards. 'President Donald J. Trump' is a formulation that never loses its surprise, and even now, halfway through Trump's first term in office, you can find yourself marvelling at the transition between the Trump of the past (*Apprentice* host, sometime professional wrestler) and the Trump of the present (leader of the free world). Friends describe being struck by the knowledge while washing dishes, standing paralysed as water runs into the sink. Some wake up oblivious, begin the day and then stumble on the real-isation, a pattern familiar to the bereaved.

In some quarters, say academia or the liberal media, Donald Trump's presidency really has been a bereavement, a sense of loss far deeper than a lost vote. One American political commenta-tor told me privately that he believed his career had been a waste of time, and confessed he'd spent the late months of 2016 play-ing video games with his son. ('Salman Rushdie finished *Super Mario World* when he was on the run,' I said, trying to cheer him up.) Sections of the American left, always suckers for paeans, have turned permanently elegiac, sandwich-boarding the end of decency and dignity, the loss of hope and truth. Social media is rife with liberal chancers who perform these rages and sorrows as ably as professional mourners.

Many fixate on the immediate fact of Trump's election. They want not a rematch but a do-over, based on a magical logic: if Trump had a *deus ex machina* route to the presidency, then he can exit it the same way, accelerated by impeachment or declared incompetence. Donald J. Trump might have generated scandals his whole life (so many they somehow cancel one another out), but perhaps this time the bill is too big to skip, and what happened in a moment on 8 November 2016 can be undone in another.

Along with Trump himself, and Hillary Clinton, and a few million other people, I happened to be in New York City for that day, and I can still remember the prematurely celebratory mood in the morning, when a Clinton win had been pencilled in. New York City hates Donald Trump: beyond its affiliation as a deeply Democratic town, he is an unwanted by-product of the place, a rag-bag of its worst qualities, Manhattan vulgarities and Queens insecurities. His comeuppance, overdue, was finally scheduled.

That was what most observers were predicting, myself included. I had heard Trump's 'grab 'em by the pussy' comments and assumed that they marked the end of his campaign. I had watched him tell lies in real time: at a New Hampshire rally inside a sportsdome, he instructed police to lock out an imaginary crowd of latecomers (I had arrived late, and fought my way through an empty car park). I could not reconcile these cheap tricks with the presidency. There was a quickening undertow, though, and fresh off the campaign trail I wasn't the only one thinking that I might have missed something.

The evening was unforgettable. For me, it rolled out in a series of bad-movie coincidences, snatches of eavesdropped conversation at newsstands ('... from rural Maryland and she said she didn't know a *single person* voting for Clinton, not one') and on subway cars ('... they'd drawn swastikas all over it. All over the maps!'). Outside the Trump International Hotel & Tower, concrete barriers were stacked but not deployed, and it wasn't until the booth results from Florida started coming in that the city really felt unsettled. Walking to Lincoln Square, I spent a few minutes checking the numbers on my phone, and then looked up to discover three or four thousand people standing just paces away, stunned into silence. An NYPD officer said it was the quietest, most docile crowd that size he had ever seen.

Soon that crowd would disperse (the silence, though, stayed over the city for days). At Clinton headquarters, the staff were said to be in tears, but the candidate wouldn't come out. I saw Michael Moore getting into a black SUV, his face ashen. Times Square was empty then, apart from some windborne trash and a few stragglers. A gathering watching a store-front TV turned out to be exquisitely diverse: a gay Clinton campaigner who had

fled the cry-in, an African-American veteran, a once-Republican
Filipina migrant. They stood, curious, in the growing cold
as Trump took to the stage. It should have been all triumph;
instead, he was upstaged by Mike Pence, whose face was trans-
mitting undisguised panic through the window.

Across the square, a posse of drunk frat boys in MAGA caps
announced themselves loudly, and our little group flinched. The
response was so instinctive, the intimidation so visceral, that I
thought I could feel the country altering minute by minute,
a change as tangible as the dropping temperature. This was the
sharp, leading edge of the Trump presidency. It was not until days
later that I recognised this feeling of incipience for what it was:
wrong. These election-night episodes weren't portents, they were
echoes. The Trumpian elements in America might be emboldened,
but they hadn't just arrived. This was not the moment 'everything
changed' at all. It was a culmination, rather than a beginning,
and the change had started months – maybe even years – before.
It was the product of other people, and other places.

At first glance, Trump's America did not look any different.
At the cheerily paranoid airport in Los Angeles, the Department
of Homeland Security agent said, 'Sell it to me,' as though I were
going for a role, not attempting a border crossing. The streets
were still wide, the Best Western breakfast buffet was still reliant
on disposable cutlery. What had changed was the mood. There
is, in political reporting, a rough correlation between proximity to power and certainty, and that relationship had begun to
break down. Instead there was a quality that a Trump supporter
speaking to *The New York Times* named 'motion sickness'. The
Axios reporter Jonathan Swan, unusually well-connected to the
administration, half-joked that he should attach an asterisk to

every White House story he wrote, reading '*This will probably be wrong in two hours.'

What sort of asterisk is needed, then, for two years, or twenty? I could only report what I saw, without any claims to special access, or even affinity. Conservatives are big on the shared mores of the Anglosphere, but as an impious, informal and mildly socially democratic Australian, American values feel strange to me as often as they feel familiar. Perhaps most jarring – and in that there might be a clue – is the absence of an American language of failure. This is a country providential in its founding and prodigious in its conception. Until now, it has believed itself exceptional in theory and practice.

When Trump voters angrily repudiated free-trade deals and wars in the Middle East they had voted for previously, at first it seemed like a paradox. After all, hadn't they voted for these things in the first place? But it's not really so inexplicable: they had entered these conflagrations expecting to win. We were now bearing witness to America's enraged and sometimes dangerous reconciliation with these failures.

The real story in Trump's America was not the change, but the continuity. Fixating on the character of the president offers a kind of perverse comfort to his critics, a Not-So-Great-Man theory of history that confines a national pathology to a personality defect. A core of 42 per cent of Americans thought he was doing a good job. If POTUS is chaotic, then he is chaotic in a way that reflects authentically the feelings of the people who elected him. He represents not a dark, new America, but the resurgence and recurrence of an old America, and the familiar crudities and cruelties that come with it. Right or wrong, that was the America I had entered as well.

DRINKING IN THE SWAMP

As happy hour starts in Bullfeathers, there are still six workers with laptops set out along the long counter, and half the busy conversation is into phones. It is a bar favoured by Washington lobbyists – 'bullfeathers' was Teddy Roosevelt's preferred substitute for 'bullshit' – but even if you missed the entry-level cynicism of the name, the crowd soon advertises its meretriciousness. It's not just the obnoxious accoutrements: the pantsuits and execu-leisurewear, the acres of plaid, even a rare matching pen-and-tie-clip in the wild. It is the obliviating way these people drink.

Lobbying has been called the most despised profession in America, and it's a close neighbour to many of the other untouchable castes: lawyers, journalists and politicians (some unlucky souls spend time in each of these circles of hell). Lobbyists, though – even politicians look down on them, and here they come to commiserate and douse their self-loathing with misty glasses of the awful house white. A grimacing barman called Kevin asks if I'd like to try some, pouring it sommelier-style into a plastic cup. It's the colour of a failed urine test, and as sweet as Scottish soft drink, but the oil men and defence contractors here drink it by the fridge.

Back when Trump was still campaigning, there were worries he might curb the excess of lobbying as part of his swamp-draining efforts. Instead, his modest reforms were soon diluted by a deluge of new money – at least US$3.37 billion in 2017 alone, and by some estimates, more than US$9 billion. One University of Kansas study found that firms availing themselves of this leverage enjoyed a 22,000 per cent return from kickbacks or beneficial regulation. Legislation is proving harder to pass in this era though, and adding to the tension in Bullfeathers is uncertainty. In Washington, the new ethical environment is confused and subject to presidential caprice, and if the Grand Old Party loses the House in November, many of these people will lose their jobs as well.

They are also just out of the orbit of real sway. The current crop of Republicans, like their leader, prefers the trappings of power garish and obvious (I even caught one influence-hawker at the front bar of the Trump International Hotel; 'just being a cliché, in the lobby,' said the prim little man). Bullfeathers is some distance from that.

'It's more down to earth. It's more real. You can find a real friend here, you know?' said a woman who spruiks billion-dollar naval weapons systems, convincing neither herself nor me. 'It's not as pompous as K Street.'

K Street, like Fleet Street, is a metonym that has lived on past a change of address. Once home to all the big lobbying powerhouses, you can now walk it and see only anonymous commercial buildings, the serifed fonts of power stripped from their windows. The law firms and 'consultancies' that specialise in pay-to-play are more diffuse and better hidden, scattered all over the city, or without real offices at all. Some of the less-connected hopefuls loiter around government buildings; others canoodle with politicians at fundraisers in bars and restaurants. Bullfeathers' proximity to Capitol Hill means politician sightings: the young Republican representative Duncan Hunter passes wearing a fanny pack, and runs a gauntlet of mockery into a waiting Jeep Sahara. 'You should google him,' someone says. 'He's a joke.' He is also the subject of a live criminal investigation into campaign finance violations and, as it turns out, just a month or two away from indictment.

The credit cards are getting a workout. I speak to a ruddy Texan from the American Petroleum Institute, who is watching the Golf Channel on mute. It turns out he lives in the Watergate Building. They didn't change the name? 'Oh, no. In fact, they make a thing out of it. When you call reception and they put you on hold, they play the Nixon tapes.'

Someone else is wearing a club tie emblazoned with silhouettes of jets. It is shape of the F-35, 'the plane that cost more than Australia', set to be the first trillion-dollar program in Pentagon history. 'Well, those skies won't dominate themselves!' he says, swinging a pint of IPA like it is a tankard.

I speak to another petroleum flack, a coiffed gourmand who blogs under the pseudonym 'Hungry Lobbyist'. He rates his own drunkenness as a two out of ten, but looks more like a two out of three, and we talk steak.

Washingtonians tend to moan about the city's reputation for steakhouses. It is outdated, they say (although a 2015 *Washington Post* article outlining this backlash noted that regardless, eight new steakhouses had opened in a year). So when

I ask the Hungry Lobbyist to arrange a power lunch at a steakhouse, he chafes. 'Just a heads-up, we typically hate the phrase "power lunch" in DC,' he emails later. 'There are soooo many amazing restaurants in epic neighborhoods, but since they are off the beaten path, no politicians, etc. go there.' He distinguishes between restaurants where no one is wearing a tie and restaurants where everyone is wearing a tie, and I choose one of the latter: Joe's Seafood, Prime Steak & Stone Crab, very close to the White House.

The template for this style of carnivorous Washington establishment was set by Capital Grille, which opened in the 1990s under a manager named Tom Smitherman. I call Smitherman, and he tells me how back then, steakhouses became synonymous with Newt Gingrich's Republicans, who were riding anti-PC sentiments to take the House. 'It was very fashionable, this disdain,' he says. 'The "greed is good" mentality.' A New York Times article from 1996 describes Smitherman blowing cigar smoke in diners' faces. Lobbyists lobbied him as well, offering tips for the best tables, and he could track the rise and fall of their fortunes by whom they dined with, and how often. The best seldom dined at all.

The key, he feels, is the clichés: the mahogany and marble; the samey menus, in their own way as predictable as McDonald's. 'It's not where someone goes for an educated diner's experience,' he says. 'The cliché is endorsed because that's how it's always been done. The steakhouse is as important as any other political arena.' In his book The Lobbyists, the former Washington Post reporter Jeffrey Birnbaum recounts the history of Washington's first 'King of the Lobby', the nineteenth-century fixer Samuel Ward, who said that 'the way to a man's

"Aye" is through his stomach'. (Birnbaum has since become a lobbyist himself.)

The Hungry Lobbyist turns out to be a late scratching the next day, but I go to Joe's anyway, which is, like he says, 'beautiful inside'. There are Ionic columns and black leather banquettes, parlour palms and frosted windows. It is, in fact, uncannily reminiscent of another kind of adult-orientated transactional environment, right down to the private rooms, the discreet lobby, and the back entrance and elevator, and designed for the same purpose of putting a gloss of luxury on the furtive and tawdry. The newer, more modern restaurants in the 'epic neighbourhoods' have partly struggled to attract fundraisers because their wide, contemporary windows might invite assassination attempts.

There is something not just traditional, but almost eternal, about Joe's. Sinatra plays. The gliding waiters still wear dickies. A trio of old men at the bar run a Statler and Waldorf–style commentary on each guest thrown up by the TV show they're watching, which is called *Power Lunch*:

'Who the hell is he?'

'This guy's hair was completely white, and he made it golden, like Trump's.'

'I haven't seen him for ages.'

'He looks the same.'

'He looks terrible.'

Power Lunch reports that Pope Francis has made a critique of capitalism, aimed at the 'morally questionable activities of financial advisers in the management of savings'.

'He better hurry up and retire, this one,' says one of the barflies. 'They'd better work at getting that guy from New York City. What's his name? Dolan? He should be Pope.'

Cardinal Dolan once moved millions of church dollars to shield the organisation from compensation claims by child sexual-abuse victims, and the financial vehicle used to accomplish this was named 'an autonomous pious foundation'.

I'm still long-lunching at Joe's when I speak with James A. Thurber, one of the chief architects of campaign finance regulation. Campaign finance regulation is poorly enforced, he says, with understatement. He has studied lobbying in Washington for decades, and says the current environment is 'beyond the pale of anything I've seen since 1973'.

'In a democracy you used to have transparency,' he says. 'You need that for people to decide what corrupts. The pay-to-play has gotten way out of hand. Members are hustling for money. There's a quota.'

The job of a senator or a member of Congress is much closer to a telemarketer than most people think. Their parties give them a fundraising target to meet: the former representative for Florida, Republican David Jolly, for example, was told he needed to hit $18,000 daily. This may take up to six hours of phone calls every day, plus meetings with interest groups, other representatives and committees, followed by face-to-face fundraisers at dinner. The average American politician spends little time outside the company of millionaires.

The budget czar of Trump's cabinet, Mick Mulvaney, told a group of bankers that they had a 'hierarchy' back when he was in Congress. 'If you're a lobbyist who never gave us money, I didn't talk to you,' he said in a speech to the American Bankers Association. 'If you're a lobbyist who gave us money, I might talk to you.' Mulvaney's new job is supposed to involve regulating these bankers, through the Consumer Financial Protection Bureau.

'Lobbying is constitutionally protected in the name of our pluralist democracy,' says Thurber, 'but sometimes our pluralist choir sings in an upper-class voice.'

These days, the restaurants are not as important, he believes. What he calls a 'national psychosis' has taken hold. 'The norm previously among lobbyists was that you didn't lie,' he says. 'If you did, then they didn't trust you.' People like Michael Cohen, the president's disgraced former lawyer, changed that, when AT&T and other companies gave him millions in an effort to curb the president's very personal regulatory whims. 'He's not a lobbyist,' says Thurber. 'He's a fixer. It almost has a mob shake-down quality.'

It's happy hour in Joe's now, and the braying chatter is picking up as people drink half-price cocktails and boast. It is unreal that these are now the good ones, influencers whose code of shabby honour has been sunk in the brimming tide of the swamp. I feel sorry for them; almost as sorry as they feel for themselves.

DIVING TO ATLANTIS

'This man has come all the way from Australia to pay tribute to Philip Roth,' said the president of the synagogue, and I didn't have the heart to tell the truth – that I'd come to Newark, New Jersey, from Silver Spring, Maryland, four hours away, not from the other side of the world. It might have cost me a free lunch, as well as the company. There were women whose mothers had gone to the very same salon as Roth's mother, and a convivial local history buff named Rob Steinbaum, who was planning a tour of Roth-related landmarks. He had the decency to mistake my arrival for a sign. It helped that I wasn't the only ring-in at the service: there was also a tweaker, drawn in by the singing, who stood twitching politely in the pews until the ark doors opened, and he looked on the Torah scrolls with beatific awe, having his own high holy day.

Philip Roth had died in the middle of National Masturbation Month, which was appropriate; going to temple for him was not. Rob said that a few years ago Roth himself had guest-starred on the Roth landmarks tour, riding on the bus with everyone else.

He wouldn't set foot in a Newark synagogue though, joking instead that he would sneak back that night and set it on fire. This allergy to religious Judaism has persisted into the afterlife. 'He has asked,' Rob said, 'to be buried in a college cemetery in Connecticut.' Ground doesn't come much more goyishe.

Readers outside America tend to think of Roth as a New York-ish novelist, without drawing the distinction between Newark and New York, or even New York and New Jersey. But those differences are the key to his literary territory. Unlike New York, the Newark he grew up in was suburban, assimilatory and anti-cosmopolitan. 'Jewish parents and their children at the southwestern corner of New Jersey's largest city talked to one another in an American English,' he wrote in *The Plot Against America*. Not 'like the dialects famously spoken across the Hudson by our Jewish counterparts in the five boroughs'. Far from the Manhattan literati, the number of books in his childhood home ranged from none to three.

Before leaving, I'd been talking to my Maryland landlady about Roth. 'I'm a New Jersey Jew too,' she said, after hearing the news of his death. 'The difference is that I got over it.' Perhaps Roth 'didn't get over it' the way John Updike didn't get over Massachusetts, or James Joyce didn't get over Dublin, but these analogies don't get at the weird proximity of his half-exile. The equivalent would be Joyce writing *Ulysses* in Wicklow instead of Zurich. Only a river separated Roth from his birthplace, and it was destruction, instead of distance, that stopped his return. Other cities burned in race riots during the 'long, hot summer of 1967', but few burned with the heat that enveloped Newark. Roth's appointed biographer, Blake Bailey (he fired the first guy), told me the place Roth remembered is as vanished as Atlantis.

The 'appetite' Roth found is still there, though: dangerous and creative, wounded and resurgent, Newark is also cheerfully corrupt. 'That's impressive,' I said, pointing to City Hall's golden dome, as Rob took us touring. It was, he says, a 'gift' from a grafting businessman, and calling someone an 'indicted New Jersey mayor' is almost a tautology. Those streets where the riot started are still hollowed half a century on. I saw a member of a black church called the 12 Tribes of Israel holding a sign that read 'America's Destruction is at Hand'. The 'again' was implied.

Washington Park, mentioned in *Goodbye, Columbus*, is still there, so too the 'tragic and fatherly' Lincoln statue from *I Married a Communist* and *Portnoy's Complaint*. But the citizens who peopled Roth's world are gone, out to the Jersey suburbs. Only three synagogues retain congregations, and his childhood suburb, Weequahic, lost all but 500 of its 30,000 Jewish residents in less than thirty years. His house – now covered in eyesore crazy-stone cladding – stands on a corner renamed Philip Roth Plaza. A woman called Rhonda Hughes lives there. She prefers Ralph Ellison to Roth, but is patient with stickybeakers: Scandinavian documentary-makers, lesser writers, tourists too nervy to get out of the car.

'My friend went to Weequahic High,' she says, 'and she remembered Philip Roth because they'd studied a book about masturbation. I was like *masturbation*, really? In English class?' A woman on a Roth tour would not look into the basement windows, because, she said, she 'didn't want to know what went on in there'. That's the legacy of *Portnoy's Complaint*, some-times called the best novel about masturbation ever written. (What is, I wonder, the second-best novel about masturbation ever written?) After fifty years, Roth's book is still an isolate, and made its author so famous he joined the American Literary Recluses Society involuntarily. J.D. Salinger never had people shouting 'Get your hand off it!' at him on New York City streets.

Portnoy's Complaint had as much in common with stand-up comedy as literature, and the defence of 'literary merit' meant it could be filthier, too. Even the censor who banned it in Australia admitted it was an 'excellent satire'. Lenny Bruce and co. now sound like not-so-excellent satire, so hip they could be speaking another language. Roth found an argot that lasted almost too well, a universal tongue to describe the kind of desire so abstracted it collapses in on itself. Like Jerry Lewis, Roth is big in France, where it's hard to tell where literature ends and middle-aged male horniness begins.

His fame in the 1960s and 1970s was sex fame (and self-sex at that), one of the worst kinds. He dedicated the rest of his writing life to building a reputational counterweight to The Book of Onan, so shoring up a different sort of seminal status. And what dedication – Roth had a sense of industry and asceticism it might be better for other writers never to find out about. 'Fifty years in a room silent as the bottom of a pool', he called it. Thirty-one books, many of them composed at a stand-up desk, with a regimen that at one stage involved shouting 'Attack! Attack!' into a mirror. Otherwise, you felt, his place in the literary pantheon might have been up the back, wearing a raincoat.

A variant masturbatory strain persisted in the books, some critics thought. 'He had a kind of fetish for what men do when there's nothing else to do,' his friend Liz Del Tufo told me, and his self-exploration could feel as muggy as basement windows. There were periods thick with the squalid confines of alter egos, and the women they don't get along with. At the peak of auto-scrutiny, Philip Roth published an interview of Philip Roth interviewing Philip Roth.

There was enough recursion that even the books themselves got thinly veiled autobiographies: *Portnoy's Complaint* became *Carnovsky* in the Zuckerman trilogy. In *Zuckerman Unbound*, the second in the trilogy, the Jewish admonition 'you're killing your father' becomes so literal that Zuckerman's dad reads *Carnovsky* in hospital and kicks the bucket, the word 'bastard' on his lips. 'You have killed him, with that book,' says Zuckerman's brother. But back in real life, Roth senior was handing out autographed copies of *Portnoy's Complaint* to complete strangers – signed by himself, 'Philip Roth's father, Herman'.

It was Herman, not Philip, who took the title 'the bard of Newark'. 'That really rich Newark stuff isn't my story – it's his,' Roth recounted in his memoir, *Patrimony*. Roth said that his 'foot-soldier' salesman father 'brought Newark into our house every night':

> He brought it in on his clothes, on his shoes – literally on his shoes. He brought it in with his anecdotes, his stories. He was my messenger out into the city … *You mustn't forget anything* – that's the inscription on his coat of arms. To be alive, to him, is to be made of memory – to him if a man's not made of memory, he's made of nothing.

Roth conceded that his own memory of childhood was no richer than anyone else's; the difference was that he had Charles Cummings. Cummings, a local historian and self-described 'Newarker by choice', knew every secret of the city, and acted almost as a location scout for the novelist. He would provide research files, investigate glove factories or find a vintage photo of a policeman's buttons to furnish a description. The two walked together often, sometimes into the sort of neighbourhood where visitors get asked if they're lost.

Rob Steinbaum takes me to visit the statue of Cummings in a city park, where Roth's eulogy for his friend is set in stone. 'One hot day,' Rob says, 'Roth told Charles that he was panting so much that he needed to lose weight. "If you lose 50 pounds, I'll buy you a fancy suit," he told him. And Charles did it.'

'So did he buy the suit?' I asked.

'No. And he must have felt guilty, because he gave a big cheque to help build the statue.' Today, also a hot day, a home-less man has placed ranch dressing and a salt-and-pepper shaker on the plinth in accidental tribute.

It was memory that made Roth retire in 2013. At eighty, he realised that he could no longer carry a book in his head, and so became a prolific and ranging reader instead. Helen Garner was one of the last authors he read, and he read her with admiration.

But before then, just before he retired, the day the plaque on his old house was unveiled, there were doubts whether the at-times curmudgeonly Philip would show. He not only came, but came in a limousine, Charles Cummings in tow. Sharpe James, then the mayor of Newark, read this passage from *The Counterlife*:

> If you're from New Jersey ... and you write thirty books, and you win the Nobel Prize, and you live to be white-haired and ninety-five, it's highly unlikely but not impossible that after your death they'll decide to name a rest stop for you on the Jersey Turnpike. And so, long after you're gone, you

may indeed be remembered, but mostly by small children, in the backs of cars, when they lean forward and tell their parents, 'Stop, please, stop at Zuckerman – I have to make a pee.' For a New Jersey novelist that's as much immortality as it's realistic to hope for.

For the mayor, the recital became a party piece, performed for just about anyone who walked through his office door (at least until he was convicted of fraud). But on the unveiling day, at this first reading, Roth, who had again narrowly missed out on the Nobel Prize for Literature, listened. He was moved. 'Today, Newark is my Stockholm,' he said to those gathered, 'and that plaque is my prize.'

He is Newark's prize too, and some immortality, New Jersey-style, is fitting for a man made of memory, now made of nothing.

CHRIST ON A BIKE

I n the wave of public eulogies for Philip Roth, one of his quotes found a wide currency. It is about prescience and idiocy. 'Any satirist writing a futuristic novel who had imagined a President Reagan during the Eisenhower years would have been accused of perpetrating a piece of crude, contemptible, adolescent, anti-American wickedness,' the author stated, 'when, in fact, he would have succeeded, as prophetic sentry.' Although he said this in 1984, it was treated as a remarkable foreshadowing of the Trump presidency, and of the 'Western farce of media stupidity and cynical commercialism – American-style philistinism run amok' (also Roth) that we experience now.

It reminds me of another unexpected development: the foremost conservative intellectual in America right now is a Jungian self-help author fixated on crustaceans, who can't say if Jesus existed. Who had that in the sweepstakes? But we must believe: Jordan Peterson is for real, and he was definitely not foretold in prophecy.

For the uninitiated, Peterson is a Canadian psychology professor who combines criticism of 'social justice' with studies of atavistic myth and biological dominance hierarchies, finished with a patina of bromides: stand up straight, clean your room, etc. He is not an entirely unfamiliar figure – Peterson is heir to a tradition of centre-right commentators who take aim at campus leftists, the radicals who are shitting (sometimes literally) on Western culture. First came William F. Buckley Jr, then Allan Bloom, then Harold Bloom, then Peterson. In style, Peterson is reminiscent of his tweedy, chat-show-friendly forebears. In substance, he is such a radical departure that it borders on the bizarre.

Imagine telling William F. Buckley Jr that faith in Christ is an evolutionary adaptation on par with big testicles, as well as harmonious with Jungian archetypes, and that this, not divine revelation, is what makes Christianity 'true'. He would have socked you. Many constituencies can bond over right-on students being annoying – they are, after all, very annoying – but for conservatives, libertarians and assorted internet idiots to look to mystical psychoanalysis for a defence of rationality and science, something major must have changed. Specifically, something major must be missing.

Faith is part of the answer, but more fundamental is a deep failure of the education system. As schools and colleges become dedicated to 'workplace preparation', it is possible for educated people, even university-educated people, to encounter almost no philosophy or difficult literature at all, not even by osmosis. It wasn't Peterson's writings that made him famous – he released his first book, *Maps of Meaning*, to near anonymity in 1999 – it was his refusal to use transgender pronouns under compulsion. The 'anti-PC' types that flocked to him just had so little other cultural ballast that they signed on for the lot. Come for the transphobia; stay for the Jung. I'm no expert, but I believe psychologists refer to this kind of wholesale purchase of ideas as 'commitment and consistency': the tendency to take on beliefs not incrementally, but as a box set.

It's clear that Peterson isn't much of an expert, either. Many philosophers and thinkers have taken issue with postmodernism, lots of them on the left. Few have called on Nietzsche, Heidegger and William James (all proto-postmodernists) to do so. The professor and his followers are exercised by the idea that truth is built on a shifting ideological foundation – 'cultural Marxism', they call it – but there is nothing inherently Marxist or even radical about this idea. Instead, it is a mainstay of the 'classical liberal tradition' they claim to represent. It was Hayek, not Foucault, who said 'without a theory the facts are silent', but the two had enough in common that the French critical theorist could recommend the Austrian economist to his students.

There is a lot that is benign and even beneficial about Peterson – at heart he is really a kind of Alain de Botton for incels – but pity any professional philosopher he or his acolytes encounter. Where do you start with the 'idea' that Foucault, one of history's best-known gay academics, invented postmodernism because he couldn't get a girlfriend? Or that Christopher Hitchens, one of the few people who really could be called a 'cultural Marxist', would have been all aboard this weird mythomaniacal bandwagon? Partly because it is so diffuse, Peterson's thinking invites all kinds of strange comparisons, running all the way to Nazism. But it reminds me of something quite different: if Peterson's fans ever want to know what they sound like to a humanities graduate, they only have to speak to a Scientologist about psychology or psychiatry.

Scientology considers the contingent and complex disciplines of psychology and psychiatry, and sees not tentative answers to difficult questions, but a vast conspiracy. This conspiracy, they insist, has broad social consequences. Most importantly, it impedes the expression of an authentic self, a self that can be authored through fancy to-do lists, bootstrapping and a Manichean framework based in fantasy. To save civilisation, first you have to save yourself. This is not unfamiliar.

Perhaps it's no accident that a psychologist is making such a spirited defence of reason, logic, data and fact at the precise moment that psychology and psychiatry hit such deep trouble on those fronts. It's no exaggeration to say that the last decade has been a disaster for these fields: we now know that up to half of all history's psychology experiments have had non-reproducible results. A survey of 2000 psychologists found that 'the percentage of respondents who have engaged in questionable practices was surprisingly high' – almost 50 per cent. In psychiatry, the controversies over the specialty's 'bible', the *Diagnostic and Statistical Manual of Mental Disorders*, hit existential levels, with even the book's former author questioning the premise of a glovebox manual for diagnosing mental illness. But hey, Peterson seems to say, at least these troubled disciplines aren't the humanities.

Collectively, often painfully, many branches of psychiatry and psychology have had to recognise the huge distortions that cultural expectations and institutional norms create in their work. Too often reward and status, not data, determines the 'reality' that experiments unveil. The fifth edition of the *Diagnostic and Statistical Manual of Mental Disorders* turned out to be not exhaustive but exhausted, a bureaucratic and political beast as much as a scientific one. These disciplines had to admit the bitter lesson that inquiry is not a static process but a volatile one, where subject and object can change each other during the act of inquiry. In other words, postmodernism had its revenge.

What those on the political right have missed about post-modernists (mainly because they haven't read them) is that these writers are more often describing something than endorsing it. When the French situationist Guy Debord looks at the sunless horizon of alienation left behind by the eclipse of meaning, he's not in a deckchair drinking a cocktail. He is saying that this is just how things are now, so we'd better get on with it. 'The reigning economic system is a vicious circle of isolation,' he writes in *The Society of the Spectacle*. 'Its technologies are based on isolation, and they contribute to that same isolation. From automobiles to television, the goods that the spectacular system chooses to produce also serve it as weapons for constantly reinforcing the conditions that engender "lonely crowds".' Peterson's fans identify with the lone hero not because they are heroes, but because they are alone.

This era's most powerful man is a former reality-television star. The show he starred in did not depict reality at all, but was selectively edited, often to make sense of the star's whims: firing someone because they had a moustache, say, or looked like someone who just should be fired. The most significant influence on this man is a television show, *Fox & Friends*, that is both a reflection and an instigator of his whims. When this man wants to understand an issue, he will stage his own version, having his staff perform the role of talking heads, sometimes arguing from positions they may disagree with. Just for the show.

Pastiche, simulation – these are not arid philosophical concepts, but our world. When someone says there are multiple versions of the truth, they are more likely to be Trump's press secretary than some French egghead. But Peterson seems much less concerned with these epistemic threats outside the academy, a curious triaging that makes it hard to parse between the justice of 'dominance hierarchies' and the injustices of blunt domination.

A SHOOTING IN ANNAPOLIS

Joshua McKerrow was driving towards Baltimore when word of the shooting reached him. He had spent the morning taking photos of Navy cadets in Annapolis, and was on the way to celebrate his daughter's birthday when his editor, Rick Hutzell, called. Hutzell could not reach anyone in the newsroom of the local paper, *The Capital*, he said. Just then a stream of emergency vehicles – 'nothing but emergency vehicles', McKerrow said later – screamed past in the opposite direction, and his heart sank. McKerrow called his father and said, 'Tell Mom I wasn't there,' then turned around. When I met him, he was red-eyed and taking photos from behind the police tape, covering the killings of his own colleagues.

It was not the first shooting McKerrow had covered. Four months earlier, in March 2018, he had taken photos at Great Mills High School over in St. Mary's County, Maryland, where a student shot a fourteen-year-old and a sixteen-year-old with his father's 9mm Glock handgun. Some of those photos show school buses lined up alongside a police car, in the rain. Only the shooter had been killed, shot dead by an armed and uniformed 'resource officer' stationed at the school. In Annapolis, locals recalled the episode, but no one I spoke with could remember the school's name. Shootings with only two victims receive curt national coverage now, and the St. Mary's incident was newsworthy mainly for how brief it was. It was over in less than one minute; the resource officer had been trained to engage a gunman without waiting for backup. The shooting at the offices of the Capital Gazette – the organisation that publishes *The Capital* and *Maryland Gazette* – lasted just two minutes, and police arrived on the scene in sixty seconds. By then, five people were dead.

The local emergency services were close by and well prepared. Only six days earlier, the personnel had participated in a drill at a local high school, where an actor played an active shooter, and other actors played gunshot victims, complete with chest, limb and belly wounds rendered in make-up. The emergency-services workers who arrived at the Capital Gazette office at number 888 Bestgate Road performed a manoeuvre taken exactly from the drill: stepping over a prone body to apprehend the perpetrator. The shooter was hiding under a desk, as though mimicking the survivors.

One of those shot and killed in the Capital Gazette building, a features writer named Wendi Winters, had participated in a different active-shooter drill, held three weeks earlier at the Unitarian Universalist Church of Annapolis. She had been part of its congregation for many years. It is not known if the church drill contributed to a decision to confront the shooter, but her colleagues heard her scream 'No!' – one of them described it as 'real loud, like a fighting "no"'. Winters had once simulated a heart attack and taken an ambulance ride for a story so that she could better understand what things were like at the epicentre of an emergency.

Another victim, Rob Hiaasen, one of *The Capital*'s editors, was also celebrating a birthday: his wife's. He had given her a present that morning and told her to wait until he was home to open it. She has found herself unable to open it since.

Hiaasen was the brother of the novelist Carl Hiaasen. In February 2018, responding to the shooting at Marjory Stoneman Douglas High School in Florida, Carl had written in his *Miami Herald* column, 'By now, each new horror story arrives with a crushing familiarity, capped by the same pathetic, canned responses from do-nothing political leaders. After every bloodbath, they recycle a well-practiced script.' The script was repurposed for a bloodbath that killed his brother.

Gerald Fischman, *The Capital*'s leader writer, was a dry eccentric who used a hand-held clicker to count the words in his editorials, and surprised everyone with a mid-life marriage to a Mongolian opera singer he met online. Part of his job involved writing the editorials after shootings. He wrote an editorial titled 'Without Hope, the Violence Has Claimed Us All'. He wrote that, 'Words will not prevent another Orlando or Blacksburg or Newton or San Bernardino.' He wrote that, 'A cynic would say words are just preparation for moving to the next horrible moment, tools to leverage this one safely into the past … Shots are fired and who hasn't asked "how many?" We are so practiced that even our sympathy is cynical.' He wrote that, 'usually these events follow a dismal pattern: an angry, unstable young man – known by family and friends to be difficult and volatile, but not necessarily considered insane or under treatment – has no trouble getting his hands on high-powered weapons.' He wrote this four months before a man exactly like the one he described killed him with a high-powered weapon.

Phil Davis, the paper's crime reporter, had been speaking to Annapolis police sergeant Amy Miguez that morning. Davis was planning a story on the complex mess of jurisdictional boundaries that culminated right outside the Capital Gazette office. That afternoon he texted her: 'Help. Shooting at office.' Miguez thought he was joking, and replied 'Call County'. Davis survived, tweeting the events immediately once he was safe, but so soon afterwards that many believed he was live-tweeting. 'There is nothing more terrifying than hearing multiple people get shot while you're under your desk and then hear the gunman reload,' Davis wrote, and trolls goaded him about not attacking the gunman. Later he added, 'You wanna know how I feel? I feel like five of my co-workers are dead and the sovereignty of several others will forever be compromised because they are now only survivors, not individuals.'

By this time, Google Maps was displaying a small red landmark about the size of a match-head at 888 Bestgate Road, marked 'Annapolis Shooting'.

The staff reporter Pat Furgurson was across the road at the mall food court. He had taken the morning off for doctors' appointments, and decided to take a leisurely lunch before work. He was having a chicken sandwich ('don't tell my wife that') when the big editors in Baltimore called, trying to hunt everyone down. At first Furgurson thought the live-shooter report must be about the old Capital Gazette office building, in town. No, the new building, the editor said. Don't go. Furgurson did go, dumping the rest of his lunch, but found the intersection cordoned off already – he could get no closer than the other side of the street. He was supposed to be writing a story about a storm-water development, and even in the aftermath, it was not one he was prepared to trivialise. 'If we don't fix the water, we're not going to have any more crabs to eat,' he said.

How long, after finding out about the shooting, had he decided that the next day's *The Capital* must come out regardless? About thirty seconds, he said. His desk was next in line.

In the mall's parking lot, Furgurson joined with Joshua McKerrow and another *Capital* reporter, Chase Cook, to begin work. Cook tweeted, 'I can tell you this: We are putting out a damn paper tomorrow.' Furgurson's pick-up truck became a makeshift office; the afternoon was becoming cruelly hot, and at least the truck was in the shade. The dozens of media arriving strung themselves out along a grassy rise across from 888 Bestgate. It was hard to make anything out, beyond the trees and the police tape and the drive-thru bank in the line of sight, so the cable shows couldn't transmit much more than a sense of immediacy. The local congressman, John Sarbanes, arrived, and said that the tragedy would have a ripple effect for days, weeks, months, perhaps years. Annapolis was a state capital but really a small town, he said. Its population was only 38,000 or so, and *The Capital* devoted pages each week to school soccer scores.

Ten different agencies had arrived, and their cars were so various and spread out it was hard to count them – I lost track at around twenty, beacons flashing, only rare single whoops from their sirens. Shooters are said to like footage of police beacons, and there were so many coloured lights that in the heat the street almost seemed festive. I had expected the press to be in sympathetic shock after an attack on their own – the president and the alt-right were being mooted as possible provocateurs – but behind the concern, there was routine. Crew cadged water, pizzas were ordered; there was even some flirting. Even the media thought the media were not special: they were late to join a community of the victimised that already extended to country-music fans and gay nightclub patrons, churchgoers praying in their pews, students at high schools and middle schools and colleges and elementary schools. Years ago, when Joshua McKerrow's father was a reporter in Ohio, he had covered an incident where a berserk policeman had shot up his station's radio room.

A photojournalist with short grey hair said he'd covered so many shootings he'd lost count. He had been working in the media for eighteen years, but the number of incidents had increased over the last five. 'Unless you're here right when it happens, you won't get much,' he said. 'It's going to be organised chaos from now on. You might see someone – maybe a relative – sobbing, screaming, making their way through.' The mall had not closed – relatives had been taken there, far away from the press. Whether they had turned off the muzak, no one knew.

You could tell the Annapolitans from their faces, and because you don't see people smoke like that much anymore. Pat Furgurson, his lip quavering, moved along the edge of the crowd, carried by commiserations and tentative questions. 'Whatever happened to peace, love and understanding?' he said.

A rumour began circulating, supposedly from 'police sources', that the shooter had damaged his fingertips to avoid identification, and that authorities had resorted to facial recognition. The crew from *The Baltimore Sun* arrived to help publish *The Capital*, which would carry five obituaries and an almost-blank editorial page when it came out the following day.

A reporter said that it was the twenty-fourth mass shooting in the United States this year. Another reporter, from a different local paper, was part of the milling group lining the road. He didn't want to be identified, he said, because his publication focused on 'hyperlocal feel-good news', and he was just aiming to answer any reader questions, to 'stop any misconceptions before they got out of hand'.

The mayor of Annapolis, Gavin Buckley, arrived. His sunburn jarred with his black tie, but he was somehow able to convey the right mix of anguish and resolve. In a TV interview I had heard him describe the active-shooter drill, the one with the make-up, as 'interesting'. There must be some comfort, I said afterwards, in knowing that you were so well prepared, that you had done everything possible, that it could have been much worse. He disagreed. There was no comfort. 'Five people are dead.'

The police officer giving the briefings knew the victims well. 'This is why cops don't live to be eighty,' he said later. 'Because we carry everyone's sorrow.'

By this time, the shooter's name was circulating. *The Capital* did not seem the right target for someone launching an assault against the Fake News Media. It was too humble, too local. The shooter had to be local as well. The officer would not say his name, though he knew it. Years before, the shooter had harassed a woman he had not seen since high school. He messaged her on Facebook, and when she gently suggested he seek counselling, he stalked her for three years, bombarding her with filth and threats and sometimes pleas for help. She was fired, likely due to a call he made to her employers. She moved states. She told law enforcement, 'He will be your next mass shooter.' She still sleeps with a gun.

In 2011 *The Capital* published an article about the case, headlined 'Jarrod Wants to Be Your Friend'. The shooter sued for defamation, which is difficult in America, and even more difficult if the allegations are true. He threatened the paper so much that the old Capital Gazette building had his picture up with instructions to call security on sight. Tom Marquardt, a former executive editor at the paper, told his attorneys that 'this was a guy that was going to come and shoot us'. The shooter had threatened judges and lawyers. The harassment victim's attorney, Brennan McCarthy, said that the shooter was the most dangerous person he had ever dealt with. 'The moment I heard there was a shooting at *The Capital*, I told my wife, "That's Jarrod Ramos,"' McCarthy said. 'It did not surprise me in the least. The only question was where he would stop by first: my house or their office.'

Shortly after the defamation case, a police report found the shooter making 'mention of blood in the water, journalist hell, hit man, open season'. On social media, the shooter repeatedly referenced the *Charlie Hebdo* killings, using a hashtag that swapped *The Capital* for the French magazine: #jesuiscapgaz. In tabled court documents (he represented himself), the shooter swore a 'legal oath' to kill a writer at the newspaper. 'As of this writing *The Capital* will not pursue any charges,' Officer Michael Praley concluded in the report. 'It was described as putting a stick in a beehive which the Capital Newspaper representatives do not wish to do.'

All this predated the suspect's legal purchase of a 12-gauge pump-action shotgun. A shotgun is an unusual weapon of choice for a shooting, and it was likely used, I was told, because Maryland's gun laws are so strict. In another state he could have purchased a handgun, or a centre-fire semi-automatic rifle, but in Maryland citizens subject to a protective order, or with a history of violent behaviour against themselves or others, are entitled only to a 'long gun'. Once they purchase it, they can carry it openly on the street. If the shooter had approached 888 Bestgate Road carrying his shotgun, he committed a crime only at the moment he pulled its trigger.

The press conference to name the victims was held so close to the road that the revving of engines made it hard to hear. Afterwards, a Spanish photojournalist took me aside, as if he was going to show me something dirty. Did I know, he asked, if the bodies were still inside? His editor wanted a shot of them being taken out – a photo of 'the man carrying the bodies' was the way he phrased it, as though they would be cradled in someone's arms. I said I didn't know. It was hard to imagine they would be, given the weather: even on the brink of nightfall, the warmth made you forget about the possibility of air-conditioning. The photographer's request seemed obscene, but I wondered if the absence of bodies and blood in media coverage was any better. Probably it made no difference.

Mayor Buckley kept working. He wasn't only taking some comfort in the composure of professionalism; he was also trying to bear witness. The story could just move on tomorrow, Buckley said, and nothing would change, but that could not be allowed to happen. 'I think something has to be done,' he said. 'Because people on social media, the courage they have, the things that they say – we have to call some of that into question. The statistics that I've heard – I've heard some ridiculous numbers about how many incidents there have been this year alone … like 170 shootings. That is incredible if that is normal and that is acceptable … If progress hasn't happened, we need to hold our politicians accountable.' He kept variations of this dignified refrain going through most of the night.

'Look at that beautiful moon,' Sue O'Brien, Buckley's press officer, said. She was taking one of her only breaks of the day – to post a remembrance image on Facebook (she had known Wendi Winters for twenty-two years) – and had only just noticed the moon's brightness, brighter even than the lights shining on anchors' faces. When I saw her the next day, she had not slept.

Almost exactly twenty-four hours after the shooting, a CNN man says to me that 'the story has resolved itself', though I'm not sure why. *The Capital* is out, and it immediately becomes impossible to buy a copy. The staff talk about a second edition; there has not been one in years. The cordon on Bestgate Road is down as well, and already the glass shot out in the office doors has been replaced. People come for a closer look, not as voyeurs, but to confirm the unbelievable. They bring flowers, and someone adds a reporter's notebook. 'My doctor's office is in this building,' says a veteran, here with his son. He was at the doctor's just the day before yesterday, picking up a prescription; he keeps repeating 'just the day before yesterday'. Some time ago the veteran began casing everyday environments – banks, malls and so on – with a tactical eye, looking for the exits. He had even looked at this very building and thought it seemed an awfully soft target. 'But then I thought, the people inside are here to help people.' As we talk, a man in overalls wheels a pressure cleaner inside.

There are remembrance services. There are vigils. A crowd of a couple of hundred gather not far from the Capital Gazette office, cradling candles. 'We are not supposed to be here,' says a priest. There are at least four reverends, a rabbi and an imam, and Pat Furgurson, who is somehow there with a notebook in his back pocket, and a T-shirt that says 'Journalism matters, today more than ever'. 'We are not the enemy,' he says, referencing the president's words. 'We are you.'

There are five tolls of a bell. An Evangelical Lutheran minister says that in 2016, her church created a prayer service for incidents of mass violence. Afterwards, I ask about this, and find that most denominations have done something similar. Alongside baptism and marriage, mass shootings are now a liturgical occasion. The version on the church's website still references the Las Vegas shooting. It reads:

> With Job of old we cry out:
> Everywhere the innocent suffer.
> Our desires and efforts achieve us little.
> O God, are you good, yet do nothing to help us?
> Our answers have holes, and we fall through.

And:

> All people are grass,
> their constancy is like the flower of the field.
> The grass withers, the flower fades,
> when the breath of the LORD blows upon it;
> surely the people are grass.

And:

> God our deliverer, whose approaching birth still shakes the
> foundations of our world, may we so wait for your coming
> with eagerness and hope that we embrace without terror
> the labor pangs of the new age.

And:

> Silence follows. The silence is marked by the ringing of a bell.

The imam speaks more quietly than anybody else, and says God
does not give any man a burden greater than he can bear, but
I am not a believer.

A VERY COMPLICATED STATE

I t's difficult to appreciate, until you see it up close – say, in the confines of a Virginia high-school hall on Primary Day – how deeply eccentric the American electoral system is. Nowadays the candidates are just as eccentric, and the whole enterprise has taken on a quality that is both solemn and farcical at the same time.

Under duress, the system must be shown to work, but the electoral officials turn out to be uncertain about some of its logistics. Yes, voters have to register before they can vote in the primaries that pick the candidates. No, they don't have to vote in the same party primary that they registered for, but they can only vote once. Or once each in the senatorial primary and the congressional primary. Is that right? Even the machinery here has changed many times in just a few years: first there were tearbooks, then laptops, now iPads. But in the event of a tie (as has happened in the past), the final result relies on low-fi technology: the winner's name is plucked from a bowl.

'Virginia is a very complicated state, and this is a very complicated district,' said the precinct captain, a volunteer with a masochistic streak. 'We have a very dedicated turnout. They are mainly older voters here.' As she spoke, I watched a man, one of the oldest-looking ambulatory humans I have ever seen, make a hesitant path past the booths and towards the exit. He turned out to be Justice Anthony Kennedy, the judge who hated being called 'the swing vote' on the Supreme Court of the United States. (He is the man responsible for gay marriage becoming federal law.) Kennedy's face was an alarming colour, almost the same hue as his blue-grey suit, and some supernatural force, perhaps anxious liberal willpower, seemed to be keeping him upright. His bodyguard took him away from the media and into a car before anyone could ask whom he voted for. He was a Republican, though, or at least was put in place by Republicans, and it's hard to believe that he would cast a ballot in the congressional primary for anyone but the incumbent, Barbara Comstock.

Virginia is a 'purple state', closely contested between Republican red and Democratic blue, and moderating every year. This district, the tenth, voted for Hillary Clinton for president but returned a Republican congresswoman, a moderate who briefly criticised Trump after the *Access Hollywood* 'grab 'em by the pussy' tape was released. Ordinarily, someone such as Barbara Comstock would be safe from a primary challenger for this seat, but an effect termed 'the cult of Trump' (Charles P. Pierce, writing in *Esquire*, likened it to an infectious 'prion disease') was taking effect. Any Republicans who criticised the president, no matter how well credentialled, was at risk.

Over in South Carolina, the former governor, Mark Sanford, got chucked out of his seat for going against Trump; afterwards, he said his allegiance lay with the US flag only. In Nevada, the brothel owner and pimp Dennis Hof, star of the reality-television show *Cathouse*, became the house candidate for the party of family values, after christening himself the 'Trump of Pahrump', a nickname understood as homage rather than sacrilege.

Comstock's challenger was a long-term conservative activist called Shak Hill (his 'SHAK!' badges recalled the failed presidential run of 'Jeb!' Bush). Comstock turned up at the booth, and looked disappointed to see more reporters than voters. In fairness, it was hard to see what good talking to a 24-hour Spanish business news channel would do her, but she gave them a grab, saying (in English) that while Democrats only wanted to talk about the president, she wanted to talk about the economy. The Democrat volunteers there seemed to feel sorry for Comstock – 'she doesn't like the president, deep down,' one said – and she radiated a studied moderation that might have been less wasted in another era. One of the campaign pledges on her pamphlets was 'Stopping Congress from Using Tax Dollars for Sexual Harassment Claims', alongside endorsements from the Susan B. Anthony List, which aims to end abortion in the United States, and the National Rifle Association.

On the Democratic side, the house seat attracted six prospective candidates, four of them women, part of a groundswell of pissed-off female doctors, lawyers, scientists, veterans and women of colour, driven to politics by Trump. 'At first they were in shock, now they're animated,' a volunteer named Betsy Costal told me. She was a former lawyer brought up by New Dealer parents. 'I worked alongside Republicans in the past,' she said, 'and respected them. It's hard to imagine that happening again.'

The Virginia Senate seat was held, safely and unopposed, by Tim Kaine, the man who would have been Hillary Clinton's vice-president. But Democratic voter enthusiasm was so intense that some complained there was no one to vote for in the Senate primary, as though any vote would do.

The Republican party, realising it faced a challenge in the midterms, wanted to expend its resources elsewhere, and discouraged contestation of the Senate spot. However, the race offered an irresistible grandstand to a local county official, a racist called Corey A. Stewart. Stewart has been described as a 'neo-Confederate': he refused to condemn the Charlottesville neo-Nazi march (he called Republicans who did 'weak'), and has a hysterically expressed enthusiasm for 'Southern heritage' in the form of Civil War monuments. He is in fact from Minnesota, near the Canadian border.

Few districts in America could throw up a worse politician than Corey A. Stewart, but Virginia's tenth was exceptional in this regard. There was a bleak joke at the 2018 White House Correspondents' Dinner, where the comic Michelle Wolf said the Democrats would somehow lose by twelve points to a candidate called 'Jeff Pedophile Nazi Doctor'. At first, the independent candidate Nathan D. Larson – a self-confessed Nazi paedophile who wants to legalise incest and rape – seemed like a piece of virulent trolling, a nihilistic internet-forum prank gone wrong. But he was serious, or at least psychopathically invested in his campaign. He was also a former felon imprisoned for making threats to the life of President Obama. One curiosity of US election law: some states bar felons from voting for life, but not from seeking office.

The electoral workers in the tenth knew of Nathan D. Larson – like Corey A. Stewart, he had received international media attention – and some were waiting to see if he would reach the petition threshold of 1000 signatures to have his name put on the ballot. It was likely, but they were managing to remain professional. A Republican official called Steve Hunt seemed to be in charge. He was wearing a decrepit green suit adorned with two pins. One was Navy pilot wings ('Ever see *Top Gun*? I was the Goose role,' he said). The other was a tiny silver pair of feet – he said they were the size of a ten-week-old foetus's.

The beauty of the American electoral system, Hunt told me, was that anyone could be a candidate. 'Larson will get only as much attention as the press gives him,' he hoped, a hope that had not enjoyed good results recently.

Around the counting rooms, volunteer Girl Guides worked as runners, passing along messages from the booths. 'We think they give a community feel,' another official said. A sullen Boy Scout pushed a pallet of ballots with glacial effort. He was wearing a blue mesh workman's vest over his uniform, with 'ELECTIONS' printed on it.

By the end of the evening, it was clear that Corey A. Stewart, neo-Confederate, had won the unauthorised nomination, with a low turnout. In his acceptance speech, he said that Tim Kaine should be in jail. 'Virginia Governor Candidate Corey Stewart is Just a Guy Who Likes Free Attention', the *Washingtonian* reported. The report said that he had 'very little shot of actually winning through his love of the Confederacy'. The reports proved right, but by now America is realising that free attention ain't free.

MANNERS AND MORALS

Traditionally, racist governments have been careful to couch their legal repressions in the language of hygiene, civility or cohesion. Not so the United States when it targets Mexicans. In the past, two pieces of American immigration restriction were openly named after slurs – the Greaser Act (1855) and Operation Wetback (1954). The Memorandum for Federal Prosecutors Along the Southwest Border breaks tradition with its nomenclature, but not its nature. This was the unremarkable title Donald Trump's attorney-general, Jeff Sessions, chose for a 'zero-tolerance' approach to unlawful entries from Mexico. Migrants crossing the south-west border were to be subject to criminal, rather than civil, penalties (the action itself is misdemeanour). The memo was released on 6 April 2018, and it started causing trouble straightaway.

Thanks to Sessions, the standard punishment for first-time border-crossers changed from a fine to imprisonment. Incarcerated adults and detained children were held separately, sometimes in different states. Public outcry meant the policy was short-lived, but many of the hundreds of families treated this way have not been reunited. Some may never be.

The Obama administration also had a policy of detaining children, but it largely applied to unaccompanied child migrants. Only in exceptional circumstances were migrating parents separated from their children. This is part of the reason that the rapidity and scale of Sessions' change overwhelmed America's immigration structure so quickly.

Even when the new 'zero-tolerance policy' was in effect, the true tolerance was not zero. The Department of Homeland Security referred only around 60 per cent of illegal entries to be prosecuted, in part to avoid flooding already overburdened detention centres. Trump signed an executive order to end his own policy, while expressing his desire to remove migrants extra-judicially. He frequently changed his mind about what form this process might take. For a short period, official US migration policy was unclear, with the Department of Justice and the Department of Homeland Security not in concert.

Often, when a writer compiles an assemblage of information like this, they will add a grace note – maybe 'these facts are already well known' – to help a reader through the boring bits. There's an assumption that it might, in part, be familiar. But these facts are neither well known nor familiar. Ask Americans on the street, even news junkies, and few could outline these events with any confidence. 'What happened?' is a much harder question to answer than it used to be. The ratio of opinion to information is changing, becoming dangerously weighted to opinion. The news cycle is dominated by both interminable complicated stories and brief complicated stories. An unfamiliar concern has started to spread among professional journalists: they find themselves unable to keep up with the news, and wonder how their audiences can cope. Social media is a hindrance more often than an aid to clarity, and involves partial immersion in a hostile river of disinformation, some of it emanating from the White House.

Faced with a story of this complexity, America has retreated into antipathies. The first was anticipated, and warranted: protest and outrage at children being separated from their parents and detained. The second was less expected: the national conversation was dominated for days by a curtailed dining experience. At a restaurant called the Red Hen in Lexington, Virginia, Trump's press secretary, Sarah Huckabee Sanders, sat down with her family for a meal. They were served, finished their cheese plates and then the Red Hen's owner asked Sanders to leave. Later, the owner explained that some of her employees were gay. She believed the administration was 'inhumane and unethical', and did not want Sanders' business. Sanders complied. (The cheese plates were complimentary.)

Sanders is not the first Trump administration official targeted this way – two others were heckled out of different Mexican restaurants. There was a hint that the repugnant senior adviser for policy, Stephen Miller, the man said to be pleased with the photos of Mexican children crying, might have courted protest deliberately. Compared to the past treatment of controversial political figures – in 1972, the Vietnam War architect Robert McNamara was almost thrown off the side of a moving ferry – it is milquetoast. But the Red Hen's act of considered inhospitality (in a service environment, of all places) seemed to strike a chord, or at least ring a dinner bell, for Trump's trolls. It also gave the right wing an opportunity to counterattack.

Soon, not just the Red Hen in Lexington, but unaffiliated restaurants with the same name, were subjected to florid abuse.

A Red Hen in Washington, D.C., was egged. 'Shame on you,
Bigots and hypocrites!' wrote a woman called Connie Szczepanik
in an online review for the Olde Red Hen, an eatery in Ontario,
Canada. Trump tweeted an online review of his own: 'The Red
Hen Restaurant should focus more on cleaning its filthy canopies, doors and windows (badly needs a paint job) rather than
refusing to serve a fine person like Sarah Huckabee Sanders.
I always had a rule, if a restaurant is dirty on the outside, it is
dirty on the inside!' It is a breach of White House ethical guide-
lines for the president to target a private business, but ethics fell
by the wayside some time ago.

One of the most unsettling things for an outsider in the
United States is its vestigial puritanism. Many Americans seem
more viscerally offended by bad manners than by child concen-
tration camps, just as they are more angered by rude teenagers
than by school shootings. 'Do the kids speak to their parents
and teachers with the same level of disrespect?' Fox News radio
host Todd Starnes tweeted when Marjory Stoneman Douglas
High School students asked Senator Marco Rubio some pointed
questions. They had just survived a gun massacre, but Starnes
seemed to think it of utmost importance that they wear pencil ties. 'Parents, what would you do if your child lectured and
ridiculed a U.S. Senator on national television?' he continued.

Many of the parents he addressed objected, but in right-
wing media circles, the rudeness and incivility of those touched
by violence are often noted. This is especially true in the South,
but other areas of the country are almost equally invested in
this region's weird layer of pseudo-etiquette. In 2011, *The New
York Times* ran a piece called 'A Last Bastion of Civility, the
South, Sees Manners Decline'. It goes without saying that these

'manners' are not in contrast to exploitation and racism, but often play handmaiden to them. They are remnants of something that has almost disappeared elsewhere in the developed world: an honour code enforced by violence.

It is hugely hypocritical of Trump supporters to lecture others about incivility, but the hypocrisy is somehow frictionless. It is no longer shocking when a pimp becomes a Republican candidate. In Nevada, as already noted, accused rapist Dennis Hof, reality-television host and author of *The Art of the Pimp*, ran for office with the party's blessing, before dying mid-race. Nor is it surprising that Hof garnered the support of religious conservatives, including clergy. 'People want to know how an evangelical can support a self-proclaimed pimp,' a pastor called Victor Fuentes told Reuters. 'We have politicians, they might speak good words, not sleep with prostitutes, be a good neighbor. But by their decisions, they have evil in their heart. Dennis Hof is not like that.' Perhaps it is still eerie just how seamlessly this transition, really an about-face, has been made. The phrase 'not sleep with prostitutes' would not have been in that sentence even a year ago, but certain pastors have made their peace, untroubled by conscience.

'He is the Christopher Columbus of honest politics,' Hof said of Trump, but the new world he has opened up equates this so-called honesty with a special kind of lying. Many of Trump's own voters don't believe he is honest, but they do believe in him. They have appointed the president as a kind of proxy, one with (apparently) a genius for deals and access to the best people, so if he lies, it must be for good reason. Better to have a liar on your side than face a liar on the other. Exactly how this can operate when laws and orders and policies are issued as statements and words, in fixed form, we are still finding out. Trump often seems to believe his own falsehoods, or wants them to be true. In just a few days, the president claimed the child separations were out of his control, that his people would love them, that they were terrible and that he was responsible for ending them. As his cult-like supporters aped his changing mind, Trump even became partly right.

'It's not that I disagree about policy with Trump supporters. It's that I know they don't give a shit about policy,' the conservative commentator and Naval War College professor Tom Nichols, author of *The Death of Expertise,* tweeted recently. He had given up reasoning with the MAGA fan club. 'There's no way to have a policy argument with people whose eyes are always looking up to the television for a cue from Dear Leader about what to say next.'

In Duluth, Minnesota, a woman at a Trump rally broke down in tears when asked about the detained children. 'He just tries so hard and so many people are down on him,' she blubbered. Her tears were for her president.

POLITICAL POISON

'**I** hate shows about people who are really, really good at their jobs.' Of all the reasons to hate *The West Wing*, I haven't heard this bettered. It punctures all the hollow promise of early second-millennium technocracy, that false and shining moment where problems were mistaken as rhetorical, not material. What *Vanity Fair* called the 'Sorkinization' of politics is still in effect, and Democratic D.C. is full of staffers, reporters, advisers and others who have not just consciously modelled themselves on characters, but moulded themselves into them.

Who, then, do the Republicans imitate? If the short and inglorious career of Scott Pruitt is any guide, the answer seems to be Trump. Even in a cabinet crowded with the ethically suspect, Pruitt was a stand-out. As the attorney-general of Oklahoma he sued the Environmental Protection Agency more than a dozen times, trying to overturn the regulation of pollution. Trump made him head of the agency instead, saving him the trips to court.

Pruitt began abusing his office immediately, but so ostentatiously that the result was something like conspicuous corruption.

By the end of his tenure, the media struggled to itemise the excesses: the $43,000 secret phone booth in his office, the multi-million-dollar security detail sent to source hotel moisturiser and a Trump-brand mattress. In June, the House Appropriations Committee had to pass an amendment banning Pruitt from purchasing any pen worth more than $50; weeks later, he spent $1599.68 on eight pairs of 'tactical pants'.

Those tactical pants might indeed have been a tactic – there is a theory that Pruitt could have been trying to prove something. He is famously obsessed with secrecy (his guards followed him even within the EPA building, as though he were Darth Vader), so the fact that his indiscretions were so indiscreet makes them seem deliberate. One explanation is that he was vice-signalling, trying to prove his Trumpiness to Trump himself.

The plan backfired – Pruitt was forced to resign – but he got some of it right in the process. For one thing, he understood the essential pettiness of Trumpism. Back in 1990, the satirical magazine *Spy* orchestrated a prank in which they sent celebrities cheques for tiny amounts of money. They started with cheques for $1.11 and sent them to fifty-eight people, including Cher, Henry Kissinger and Trump. Twenty-six cashed them. They sent cheques for $0.64; thirteen cashed them. They sent cheques for $0.13; two people cashed them: arms dealer Adnan Khashoggi and Donald Trump.

This penny-pinching is not about the cash – it can't be, for thirteen cents. It's about a need to take advantage at every opportunity. The monetary miserliness is a subset of a moral miserliness built on the complete absence of kindness, humility, grace, intellect, honesty, loyalty or anything else redemptive.

Pruitt was unusual among Trump nominees for his relative

poverty – he was 'only' a multimillionaire – and he may have overcompensated, winding up a kind of nouveau-nouveau riche in the process. His actions reveal the neo-feudalism that has taken hold in America, where the struggles of the lower and middle classes are quarantined as well as overcome.

It is telling that Pruitt claimed first-class flights were necessary for security reasons. This rationale was dubious – he would stay in opulent hotels against security experts' advice, and one of the alleged threats used as justification was a magazine cover where someone had drawn a moustache on Pruitt's face. But however ludicrous his cover story, the idea that luxury is a precondition for security is widespread in America. If anything, a first-class seat rather than a charter jet is on the modest side (though Pruitt did ask about a private charter before someone put their foot down).

There is an infamous clip where the televangelists Jesse Duplantis and Kenneth Copeland compared and defended their private jets on air: Duplantis insisted that God had told him personally to buy the plane, while Copeland claimed that commercial airlines were, in this 'dope-filled world', comparable to flying in 'a long tube with a bunch of demons. And it's deadly.'

Copeland's audience members likely fly coach, if they fly at all, but in his vision they sit alongside a bunch of dope-filled, deadly demons. It is hard to see how the plebs don't take umbrage, but many of them share a belief that public space is inherently dangerous, even Satanic. There is a lower-rent version available to them as well: calling the police on black swimmers or Hispanic picnickers, Asian firefighters or young men wearing hoodies, though they must know that dialling the digits can have fatal results.

Sometimes it seems that the rich are envied most not for their cars or their lovers, but for their fences and their panic rooms, their healthcare and their schools: their safety, in other words. The richer you are, the safer you are, and any moment not spent making yourself richer is therefore dangerous.

By the time of his ousting, something strange had happened to Pruitt: he had become a source of amusement. The media called him 'ridiculous' and a 'comically corrupt grifter'; about the mattress incident *The Washington Post* reported, 'Even White House press secretary Sarah Huckabee Sanders could not suppress a wry smile last week when asked during a media briefing about the EPA chief's enlistment of a different aide to hunt for a secondhand mattress from the Trump International Hotel' to furnish an apartment used by Pruitt. 'I couldn't comment on the specifics of the furniture used in his apartment … and certainly would not attempt to,' Sanders said. Reporters laughed.

The apartment was owned by a fossil-fuel lobbyist, and Pruitt eventually skipped out on the discount rent, after which the locks were changed. When questioned on his decision to lease the residence in the first place, his reaction was feigned outrage: he was 'dumbfounded' that anyone saw an ethical issue with accepting below-market rates for a condo owned by a lobbyist who was in the middle of pushing a case he was 'regulating'.

I guess it *is* funny, this discrepancy between principle and reality. A political figure is not supposed to be corrupt, corruption is not supposed to be open, regulators are supposed to regulate. The story is also picaresque: Pruitt was making his amoral way in an amoral world, and it was only pushing things too far that stopped him getting further.

'I believe you are serving as President today because of God's providence,' Pruitt wrote in his resignation letter. 'I believe that same providence brought me into your service. I pray as I have served you that I have blessed you and enabled you to effectively lead the American people. Thank you again Mr. President for the honor of serving you and I wish you Godspeed in all that you put your hand to.'

There is talk that Pruitt may return to Oklahoma, such disgraces no longer prohibitive to a refreshed career in politics, or work as a consultant to the coal industry (he began collecting funds for his legal fees before he resigned, and energy interests gave generously). On parting, *The Wall Street Journal* began its editorial in his defence by claiming that 'the permanent progressive state finally ran Scott Pruitt out of the Environmental Protection Agency ... and the tragedy is that Mr. Pruitt gave his enemies so much ammunition'. That is more fantastical than anything in *The West Wing*.

GOAT RODEO IN HELSINKI

'You don't know what's going to come out of this meeting,' said Jon Huntsman, the American ambassador to Russia. There is fun to be had, analysing the facial expressions of Trump-adjacent officials, and when Huntsman made this statement to NBC's *Meet the Press,* he seemed to be bracing himself physically. He didn't look quite as dire as White House chief of staff John Kelly, so visibly unhappy at a NATO breakfast that an official said he must have been 'displeased because he was expecting a full breakfast and there were only pastries and cheese'. I'm sure shit sandwiches are harder to digest in the AM; Huntsman knew he would be eating his at the all-day buffet – Donald Trump face-to-face with Vladimir Putin in Helsinki, with no aides or stenographers, scheduled for ninety minutes (in the end they went over time). What could go wrong? What could go right?

It was a meeting, not a summit, Huntsman insisted, and the State Department kept repeating the distinction to reporters, right up to the moment Trump called it a summit himself. The president and his foreign policy outfit are rarely reading the same book, let alone on the same page, even if that page is physically handed to Trump. After Putin's fraudulent re-election in March 2018, Trump ignored written instructions in his briefing papers that read 'do not congratulate', instead telling the Russian president about the 'stupid people' who wrote the note. In another piece of failed pre-emptive damage control, Huntsman said the non-summit was 'to hold the Russians accountable for what they did'. He was talking, in hope, about the Russian interference in the 2016 presidential election, which had just produced another round of FBI indictments. Trump had other ideas. Invited to describe Russia's malfeasance at the press conference afterwards, he instead said, 'We're all to blame', while Putin, alongside him at another podium, did an impression of a straight face.

In the past, moments of perceived American weakness like this were named, given shorthands to aid endless repetition. When George H.W. Bush warned against 'suicidal nationalism' in Ukraine in 1991, it was tarred as the 'Chicken Kiev speech'. Barack Obama's hatchet-burying mission to Moscow became part of a so-called 'apology tour' (prophetically, when Hillary Clinton handed a red plastic 'reset' button to Russian foreign minister Sergey Lavrov, it contained a mistake: the Cyrillic said 'overload' instead). So far, most names for Trump's effort in Helsinki are unprintable, though one information security commentator called it a 'goat rodeo' and 'Yalta on ether'. It represented not just a violation of diplomatic norms, but a wake for them.

Trump's tendency to side with murderers and meddlers against American legal institutions is no longer surprising, but his manner in Helsinki was new. He was quiescent: the judo handshakes and preening walk he displayed with other world leaders disappeared, and in the presence of Putin he cut a meek figure, even glancing at the ground. In the parlance of our times (and his biggest supporters), he looked cucked. There must be few more worrying signs at State than Donald Trump having a sudden modesty outbreak. Putin is a skilled manipulator in these arenas – a former State Department official told *The New Yorker* that Trump was like 'an amateur boxer up against Muhammad Ali', and the Russian leader looked intent on not just finishing Trump, but setting a personal high score. The humiliation was so complete that the American president left Helsinki enthusing about what he called an 'interesting' offer: Russian 'investigators', Putin suggested, could assist the American inquiry into Russian electoral interference. That's quite a bonding experience.

Sergey Lavrov called the outcome 'better than super' – because even the wildest dreams don't get this wild – but American reviews were not so glowing. 'No prior president has ever abased himself more abjectly before a tyrant,' said Senator John McCain, from his deathbed. Former US ambassador to Russia William J. Burns called it 'the single most embarrassing performance by an American president on the world stage that I've ever seen'. The former CIA director John Brennan said it was 'nothing short of treasonous'. It was so bad that even sections of Fox News condemned the president. Does Putin have compromising material on Trump? The question moved into the mainstream, though there was a strong counterargument: surely a real Russian asset would be better at hiding it than this.

The former secretary of state James Baker used to talk about 'bladder diplomacy', the epic, break-free, well-hydrated meetings he undertook, some lasting almost ten hours. This brand of crude psychology, rather than the bladder diplomacy of the pee tape or any other *kompromat*, is all that's required to manipulate Trump. His mental incontinence means he can only pay attention for a few minutes, struggles with reading anything without pictures, and broadcasts his thoughts and feelings every morning. He is arrogant and insecure in equal measure, and even his allies say he makes no distinction between the national and the personal. 'I think the president has difficulty conflating how people treat him personally with representing our national interests,' said Bob Corker, the Senate Foreign Relations Committee chair. It's an extraordinary on-the-record comment, one that really means the president is an easy mark, and everyone knows it.

This malleability and tendency to distraction over shiny objects has been readily exploited. The French pioneered it – see how *The Washington Post* described Trump at a Parisian parade: 'he ... eagerly leaned forward as he took in the spectacle, frequently jostling his wife or French president Emmanuel Macron when he saw something that particularly delighted him. Whenever troops were before him, Trump jumped to his feet and applauded with an enthusiasm that exceeded the response of those around him,' the paper said. He may even have been allowed an ice-cream on the way home. Chinese president Xi Jinping reinvented a special status called 'state visit-plus' ('China Won,' read *Time*'s cover afterwards); Japanese prime minister Shinzō Abe handed over a gold-plated golf club; president of the Philippines Rodrigo Duterte laid out a 'red carpet like nobody ... has probably ever received'. Instead of challenging Manila on its policy of killing suspected drug dealers, Trump asked his staff why America couldn't do the same.

It's exactly the brash and idiotic form of 'strength' Trump supporters prize that makes their man so weak. Most of Putin's

serious domestic adversaries have also been billionaires, and he
has dispensed with them easily, so he understands the transactional mentality of mercantilism well. There are limitations to
seeing everything as a deal or a potential publicity stunt, especially when coupled with a gnawing need for affirmation. *The
New York Times* reported that Senator Mitch McConnell told
associates that Trump is 'inclined to treat criticism of Russian
meddling in the United States as giving credence to unproven
allegations that his campaign colluded with foreign actors'.
Trump has blurted out similar things to strangers on a New
Jersey golf course, and mentions his electoral win at every available (or unavailable) opportunity. Putin can have Crimea – he'll
take Wisconsin.

Russian manipulation also draws on a greater gullibility:
Trump supporters' susceptibility to disinformation. For the
GRU's flotilla of fake news to land, its operatives had to understand the wants and needs of the red states, and this cynical
view of America has proved more than half-right. Russian intelligence identified the locus of control in the Grand Old Party
as the National Rifle Association. They guessed correctly that
Trump supporters would side with white foreigners over non-
white Americans, and, according to the news and analysis site
Vox, a study of Russian-bought Facebook ads found they sought
to divide Americans on race more than on any other issue.

This alliance based on semi-latent white nationalism – you
could call it white internationalism – is not going away. If anything, the active measures were not active enough, and bots
flooding social media were often outstripped by talkback callers,
something that has continued after Helsinki. Some Trump supporters were nonplussed by the president's submissive display,

but many sounded more grateful than chagrined. One caller said to C-SPAN: 'I'll try not to sound too awful, but I want to thank the Russians for interfering in our election to stop Hillary Clinton from becoming president.' The cult is becoming a suicide cult.

Putinism is already an end point of Trumpism: the natural conclusion of constant degradation of the media, a cavalcade of lies designed to exhaust rather than to persuade, shabby national pageantry, voter suppression and open graft. The historian Timothy Snyder wrote that Putin is 'offering masculinity as an argument against democracy', and Trump is doing something similar, even if he is the smaller man. Australia's own Tony Abbott shows the reach of this approach: as prime minister he offered to shirtfront Putin, yet still regards Trump's foreign policy largely as a success, because of its stylistic muscularity. Such an approach to power is no longer a psychosexual issue to be worked out behind closed doors, but an international malaise, a global acting-out of fragile manhood.

There is an exception, though, in Trump's caricature of the American man. He is not a warrior. It's too early to talk about saving graces, and perhaps the wrong time even to mention hope. But so far, Trump's antipathy to military action seems genuine. If he breaches diplomatic protocol by breaking Washington's consensus on belligerence, the fallout is relative. He may visit calamities on his own country, but if he is too gun-shy and easily stymied to attack others, those calamities must be ranked against the consequences of another Iraq or another Libya, a new Syria or more fresh blood in Afghanistan. (Someone pointed out that after eighteen years of fighting, the Afghan war is now old enough to enlist in itself.) Trump, who is proving a president that appears strong to his base and at the same time weak to his diplomatic peers, may have found an accidental solution to the problem of American warmongering. We have already seen the result of decades of American decisiveness and 'strength projection' – isn't some incompetence at the initiation stage a welcome relief? If others count their luck and hold the peace, that really would be the ultimate deal.

THE AESTHETIC
OF THE AR-15

The expression 'guns don't kill people, people kill people' is a cliché old enough to have seeded many variations. One version of the phrase features in a National Rifle Association ad starring Stephen Willeford, who interrupted a mass shooting at a Texas church. 'It's the heart, not the gun,' he says in the spot, and he is proof: Willeford is carrying the same gun that the shooter did, an AR-15. This is not much of a coincidence – there are so many AR-15s in America that their total number is hard to estimate, but reckoned at between five and ten million. This gun, the ad suggests, did not make anyone do anything of its own accord, and offers a control group as proof.

Whatever its intention, this proposition is not quite as ludicrous as it first appears, and after firing an AR-15 myself, I began thinking about this pat expression in a different way.

The AR-15 is now notorious – the weapon of choice for mass shooters – and handling one was a bit like meeting a celebrity: the same surprise that it looked smaller in real life; the same sensation that my expectations hadn't been met, though I wasn't exactly sure how.

I won't name the US shooting range where this encounter took place – apart from some nods to state gun law, it could have been any spot in the country where paper targets are shot at indoors. If you've never been to a firing range, it is surprisingly like a bowling alley, right down to the rain-stained brutalist exterior, the lanes, the drink machines and the discount coupons, the over-the-counter hires, and merch for the more serious. There are couples on dates, and even kids, five or six years old, watching as their parents open fire.

'There is no age limit here, as long as they're accompanied by a 21-year-old,' the duty manager told me, and that's the juxtaposition that non-Americans find so odd: the mismatch between the trappings of everyday life and the present potential for violent death. At first I thought it was dealt with by a kind of naivety, by separating death and guns – to a regular shooter, fear at a gun range must seem as ridiculous as fretting about car accidents at an Avis counter. But that analogy between guns and cars as life-threatening hazards, while often made, never really works. While the relationship between shooting guns and shooting guns at people to kill them is indirect, it is never absent. Those paper targets are often shaped like people, not tin cans, and the red on the bullseye represents a human heart.

After scanning my Groupon, the guy behind the counter asked if I was alone. Some gun ranges won't rent firearms to solo shooters because of the suicide risk, though these self-shootings at ranges are uncommon (one internet post I'd seen called them 'rude'). The attendant's mild concern was not truly for me it was a worry I might become a clean-up on aisle three. I must have looked upbeat enough to arm.

I expected some safety theatre – a class of do's and don'ts or a bad instructional video – but five minutes later I had in my hand a little plastic carrier, which held a set of safety glasses, a box of ammunition and a Glock 17 pistol.

'Western man, especially the Western critic, still finds it very hard to go into print and say, "I recommend you to go and see this because it gave me an erection,"' the theatre critic Kenneth Tynan wrote, and there's a similar misgiving about writing that guns are fun (it's interesting that the Hemingway-esque gun-slinging writer is almost extinct). You can also go too far the other way: when the *New York Daily News* writer Gersh Kuntzman wrote that shooting an AR-15 had given him a temporary form of PTSD, he unlocked the peak hate-mail achievement of his thirty-year career. Right-wingers mocked his effeminacy, while left-wingers thought he was trivialising PTSD.

I didn't expect shooting to give me an erection or PTSD. In my experience, immersive research produces slow-burn insight more often than eureka moments, so this was a surprise: picking up a loaded gun in America is an epiphany. Not because it made me feel like a bigger or a smaller man, but because it showed just how much trust is involved.

America is not a high-trust society – it is polite but suspicious, sometimes to the point of paranoia. Public space is often punitive (lethally so for people of colour), and the searching worry about crime is severe enough that staying too long at a coffee shop or letting children play unsupervised in a park can become police matters. If you're white, this sensation is more cloying than oppressive, but still very noticeable.

The Glock made it disappear. The government was entrusting me with a firearm, thanks to the Second Amendment. In theory, I was allowed to fire it at anyone threatening my liberty, up to and including the police and the military. The firing range's owner was entrusting me with a gun, its manager was entrusting me with a gun. Most importantly, so too were the other shooters.

I had encountered the phrase 'responsible gun owner' countless times without a simple realisation that was now impossible to miss: when you're at a firing range, the stranger standing next to you can kill you any time they like, and you can kill them. If you're unlucky, this can happen by accident, as well as by intent. You'd better believe everyone is responsible. I have not experienced many bonds of trust more intimate, and this was a one-off trip. Repeated, I imagine it creates a communion stronger than church.

A policeman was practising his quick-draws, and I set my carrier down at the next lane. I'd taken the pistol to warm up, thinking it would be easier. This was wrong. The range was hot, and even with ear protection the Glock was so loud it was hard not to flinch before pulling the trigger. My eye protection fogged with sweat. I finished the box of 9mm rounds at least able to load, aim and fire.

There was a different man behind the counter this time, college-aged, with piercings. 'You'll find the AR a lot easier,' he said, 'and a lot more fun. It's more stable and the technique is easier.' Then he handed me a black case perhaps a metre long, and we took it into a mocked-up training lane in the lobby to have a look.

An AR-15 is hard to describe, not just because it is nondescript (you know what it looks like), but because it is made from such contested material. The most fundamental words used to describe it are debated: 'firearm' sounds a straightforward term, but legally only one part of an AR is a gun, and that is the small section with the trigger and handle called the lower receiver. The other pieces can, by law, be sent directly to your home, and it is even legal to make the lower receiver yourself, as long as you don't sell it.

The AR-15 is sometimes called a 'long gun', or an 'assault rifle', though some gun-rights activists insist there is no such thing as an assault rifle. Is it a 'military-style weapon'? It fires only one round at a time, and modern military rifles are usually fully automatic. Members of the military don't object to this description though, and the army-issue M-16, when fired in a semi-automatic mode, is functionally and tactically almost identical to an AR.

Calling an AR a 'platform' would be accurate: it is off-patent, has countless manufacturers (who call it a 'modern sporting rifle') and can be built and customised piece by piece, out of thousands of after-market parts. *Wired* magazine called it a 'gadget', and it has been compared to Lego, gaming computers and even Barbie dolls in its versatility. The NRA calls it simply 'America's rifle', partly to supersede the controversy over what AR stands for (it stands for ArmaLite rifle, not assault rifle). Calling an AR a 'black rifle' would be very accurate, and I think captures one of the key components in what an AR really is, which is an aesthetic.

Another reason the car analogy doesn't hold: a civilian version of the AR-15 has existed since 1963, when it was called the Model R6000 Colt AR-15 SP1 Sporter Rifle. Alterations since that time have been largely cosmetic (though differences in the barrel twist have changed its velocity). What model of sedan has been sold unchanged for fifty-five years? The NRA is right that the AR-15 is a constant, a control. It is the heart, not the gun.

I was conscious that the model I was about to fire, the Smith & Wesson M&P15X, had been used in several mass shootings, most recently in Parkland. The fact I knew this, and knew the names of the shooter in this and other mass killings involving the gun, felt disturbing, almost like it came with an absurd form of athlete's branding endorsement. But I also knew that ARs were rarely used in other kinds of murders. Most killings in America are committed with handguns. Fists are a more common murder weapon than AR-15s, though less effective. Some states, like Maryland, have no record of a single killing with an AR-15. This is why many jurisdictions make it harder to obtain handguns than black rifles.

All this means is that gun violence is not double-entry bookkeeping. It cannot be understood by actuarial tables. If you own a gun, you are much more likely to shoot your partner or yourself with it than an intruder. These odds fall if you are a woman, or if you are older. The ratio of guns to gun deaths is not constant, and the ratio of mass shootings to AR-15s is not constant, either. Citizens own more firearms than ever, but murders involving them have declined. America has more gun deaths because it has more guns, of that we can be sure, but then the chains of causation become more speculative and unclear.

No AR-15 or AR-15 analogue was used in a mass shooting before 1984. That year, it was used in a school shooting by a man called Tyrone Mitchell. This incident did not have the characteristics of the kind of school shooting we see regularly now. Mitchell was African-American, twenty-eight and had grown up in the Jonestown cult. His family had died at the mass suicide event in Guyana, and this seemed to have precipitated a breakdown. In the massacre, he fired the AR-15 from a window of his home, located across the street from the school, and killed two and injured twelve before shooting himself (with a shotgun).

AR shootings were intermittent for many years; then Bill Clinton introduced a federal assault-weapons ban. There's a lot of conjecture about whether this ban did anything to reduce massacres, and if it did not, there is a good reason: the thrust of the ban was aesthetic. There is another fascinating control group here – a firearm called the Ruger Mini-14. It fires the same ammunition as the AR, it can carry high-capacity magazines and its muzzle velocity is almost the same. But it was never subject to the assault-weapons ban, because it has a rifle-style rather than a pistol-style handle, and no bayonet mount. These make no difference to its ability to shoot people – and it has been used in a mass shooting in America, at the Lockheed Martin plant in Meridian, Mississippi, in July 2003, where six individuals were killed before the murderer shot himself. The Ruger is wood and chrome, and patterned like a hunting rifle. It remained legal only because it looked less menacing.

My AR did look menacing, and it was the unadorned version. On the rifle lanes, almost everyone else was shooting one as well, and theirs were all tricked up with scopes, tripods, paint jobs and the other paraphernalia of special forces, sometimes mockingly called 'tacti-cool'. It's easy to underappreciate just how nerdy gun culture is. Shooting is often coupled with fishing, and if you've fished, you recognise immediately the attention to minutiae, the mutual mansplaining, the vast folk knowledge of arcane and pointless detail. As a beginner and a stranger, the problem wouldn't be getting advice. It would be getting the stream of advice to cease.

There was a military guy at the range, but he had the air of a role-playing dungeon master, and his student, firing his AR in the prone position, was a cross-eyed nebbish. He had a higher-capacity magazine, harder to get in this state, and as we yelled our conversation over the earmuffs he called it a 'party stick'. Jesus. A lot is made of the fact that AR owners are usually white guys in their fifties who own more than one. While the racial anxiety component is real, these are also the kind of people who own model trains and tie trout flies and make furniture shaped like tree trunks. Among other things, I was about to participate in a boring hobby.

I settled my nerves, took the plastic flag out of the chamber, loaded the magazine, pulled back the charging handle, dropped the bolt and set the safety (which I must have checked at least ten times already) to FIRE. Then I pulled the trigger.

'Guns are one of the primary avenues by which ordinary Americans experience beauty,' Stephen Marche wrote in *Esquire,* though I'm not sure I would call this beautiful. It was ergonomic, though, engineered. Intent, design and result came together. It was much easier than the Glock, and seemed somehow quieter as well, because it was more controlled. It's interesting that even as a novice you can tell a bad gun – this one had a sticky bolt – and after getting two jams that spooked me, I requested a substitute. Better. By the end of the session I was hitting centre of the target every time, and congratulated myself by picking up a handful of hot brass.

The guy next to me had a brand-new shotgun, a 12-gauge bullpup. It was a gift from his brother, and I stopped to watch him fire it. A hunting gun, shooting solid slugs, it was so powerful I could feel the great roaring woof of fire and energy coming from its muzzle, though I stood several feet behind it. Sometimes, the staff told me, someone would bring in a gun so powerful its muzzle blast alone would shred the neighbouring target.

Something about proximity to the shotgun's force was a bit depressing. It wasn't that it was powerful, it was that it was so much *more* powerful than any creative force I had encountered close-up. It was stronger than love. The silence between shots felt loud.

It was also very tacti-cool. It didn't look like something to shoot a deer with, unless the deer was heavily armed and holed up in an Abbottabad compound. This was new. The manager told me that the indoor range had started to lose customers to nearby outdoor ranges, and not just because it was summer; they wanted to shoot armour-piercing rounds that would punch through the concrete walls and fly out into the parking lot. There is a stunning indicator of just how recent this development is. The biggest gun industry trade show in America is called SHOT, and as recently as 2004, AR-15 makers were banned by SHOT's organisers from displaying any 'tactical' imagery there, not because of legal necessity, but for reasons of taste. AR-15s had to look like hunting guns. Unbanned, this style of display then became the most popular, and today's hunting guns look tactical instead.

The War on Terror is a big part of why. It turned America's ever-present obsession with the military into something cultish. The assault-weapons ban was rescinded, and the AR-15 became available again, as a collector's item that could be re-banned at any time (perhaps the most powerful and unintentional 'for a limited time only' sales offer in history). That's why I was here, with a half-stoned college dropout with man bangs, talking about supercavitating ammunition.

Wound ballistics is prime real estate for the banality of evil, and I had just read a 10,000-word article about the history of the .223 calibre (a rollercoaster of bureaucratic inertia and military and scientific factionalism, as it happens), so I was keeping up. More-lethal bullets were more humane, he was saying. Just like killing an animal in an abattoir, you wanted to kill a human instantly; that way they wouldn't suffer. He was sincere. Not a bad guy, and the talk didn't make me think of children cowering behind desks or anything. That was an outlier risk, nothing to do with what was happening here or the people present. The point of a civilian owning an AR-15 was owning an AR-15.

Still, something had changed. Gone wrong, you could say. Something at the heart of things.

A CONSPIRACY
(IF YOU WILL)

O n 5 August 2018 an article headlined 'Trump tweeted what?!?' became one of *The Washington Post*'s most-read stories. That could serve as the headline for most articles, most days. The 'what' Trump tweeted was a statement seen as a fresh admission of collusion with Russia during the 2016 election campaign: 'Fake News reporting, a complete fabrication, that I am concerned about the meeting my wonderful son, Donald, had in Trump Tower,' the president microblogged. 'This was a meeting to get information on an opponent, totally legal and done all the time in politics – and it went nowhere.' *The Post* argued that 'Trump fails to understand that the very meeting he is acknowledging is collusion – or conspiracy, if you will – to break campaign-finance laws.' The former George W. Bush speechwriter David Frum tweeted a suggested 'headline' of his own: 'TRUMP CONFESSES HIS SON MET WITH RUSSIAN AGENTS "TO GET INFORMATION" AGAINST CLINTON'. But this wasn't even a headline – Trump had said much the same thing in July 2017, when it attracted less attention.

August is wildfire season in the United States, and the vast Californian blazes seem to share the same qualities as the stories about collusion (or conspiracy, if you will) that are so entrenched in the American media. They are destructive, unprecedented, but at the same time monotonous. There is a further symmetry: the right's pattern of response on collusion mimics its shifts on climate change. First, an outraged denial that such a thing could be possible. Then, the accusation of a counter-conspiracy disseminated by the media. Finally, the glib assertion that what has happened has occurred loads of times in the past, and is absolutely no cause for concern. A member of Trump's legal team, the former New York mayor Rudy Giuliani, does a kind of 'man of a thousand faces' act on cable morning shows, sometimes changing his position between spots, and occasionally unable to wait that long. On 30 July 2018, when Fox News' *Outnumbered* played a Giuliani clip from that morning, an angry Giuliani rang in to debate his own talking point.

'When I said today that there was no collusion, and that collusion also is no crime, I've been saying that from the very beginning,' Giuliani said, something he had not been saying since the beginning. 'It's a very very familiar lawyer's argument that ... my client didn't do it, and even if he did it, it's not a crime.' In other words, the president is not a crook, and even if he is a crook, being a crook is not a crime. Previously, Giuliani contravened the president's denials about a pay-off to the adult film star Stormy Daniels, in a *Hannity* interview so peculiar it prompted published speculation that the former mayor had been drinking. In Washington, pundits debated whether this brand of lawyering was best for Trump; meanwhile *Politico* reported that the president was at ease with what is called Giuliani's 'ad-hoc style'. As a defence, it was questionable. But as a tactic in the court of public opinion, it seemed to be working, and working in cahoots with Trump's own 'ad-hoc style'.

The Trump campaign's collusion with a foreign power, if proven irrefutably, will be a story bigger than the Watergate scandal. But the consequences may not end up bigger than Watergate, as veterans of that episode acknowledge. 'Nixon might have survived if he had Fox News and the conservative media that exists today,' Nixon's former White House counsel John Dean told *Rolling Stone* in July. 'I doubt Trump will be forced from office, even if Mueller has tapes of him talking with Putin about how to rig the election … And given the fact he is shameless, he will never resign.' Not only has the media environment changed, but so too has the moral environment. There's a theory that the Watergate tapes did more political damage in exposing Richard Nixon's profanity than in exposing his corruption. Today, Trump's supporters have embraced not just the 'locker-room talk', but the whole locker-room. More than campaign finance law has been violated already. A taped confession of sexual assault and harassment has been priced in, and running businesses while president has almost ceased to be a matter of controversy.

More fundamentally, what could be called the rhetorical reality is not the same. It's obvious that Giuliani's arguments make no sense, and even Trump's supporters must be aware of this. One of the less reported lines of the Helsinki conference was Trump saying 'there was no one to collude with', a philosophical claim so notional it's hard to know how to counter it. While fact-checkers dutifully award the president Pinocchios day after day, he inhabits a realm beyond their reach, speaking to an audience that doesn't care, and moreover is actively hostile to this intrusion.

The president's own grand conspiracy theory is that Obama spied on the Trump campaign (possibly with Russian assistance), then colluded with the FBI and the deep state to undermine his electoral win. It is a world where the FBI re-opened an investigation into Hillary Clinton to help ... Clinton? But even this fantasy is still too reality-based for many of his supporters. Conversations with right-wing Republican voters almost inevitably devolve into conspiracy theories, and at Trump events in Florida and Ohio, a cultish following for the internet-sleuthing 'QAnon' movement showed itself in numbers. 'We are Q' read a sign placed right behind the podium.

Calling QAnon a conspiracy theory doesn't do justice to its ambition. It is a secular cosmology, almost a secular theology, based on a millenarian belief that Trump is cleansing the world of criminal paedophile rings (of which Obama and Clinton are members), or globalists, or take-your-pick. According to its logic, such as it is, Special Counsel Robert Mueller is not investigating Trump but instead acting as a double agent, working *with* Trump to take down Clinton campaign staff, who may or may not have been working with Putin. Strangely, this does not seem to reduce QAnon's hostility towards Mueller; perhaps its adherents have to be double agents as well.

It feels almost forgotten that Trump made his entry into politics as a conspiracy theorist. His birtherism – the belief that Barack Obama was in fact a secret Kenyan citizen and therefore ineligible to be president – became mostly dormant, discarded once it was no longer expedient. Still, like attracts like: Trump hired the deep-state crank Joe diGenova to his legal team, after the lawyer promoted a Hillary Clinton collusion theory on *Fox News*. Trump's former adviser Roger Stone once claimed that Chelsea Clinton had had four plastic surgeries to hide the identity of her real father. The InfoWars host and owner, Alex Jones, propagates a belief that the Sandy Hook mass shooting was an elaborate hoax and, post-election, it was reported that the president called the broadcaster to thank him for his assistance. InfoWars fans routinely harass the bereaved parents of children killed in the massacre, accusing them of being actors.

Last year one of these parents, Leonard Pozner, gave a brutal interview to *The Guardian*, describing the aftermath of his son's death, and the delusions that had accumulated around the mass shooting. He conceded that in other circumstances, he might have believed in the conspiracy theories himself. Referencing 'pizzagate', another Clinton-centric calumny that links a pizza restaurant to a paedophile ring, he said, 'I would not have been as immediately dismissive of it, that's for sure.' He then produced a description of this moment in history that could act as its epitaph. 'History books will refer to this period as a time of mass delusion. We weren't prepared for the internet. We thought the internet would bring all these wonderful things, such as research, medicine, science, an accelerated society of good. But all we did was hold up a mirror to society and we saw how angry, sick and hateful humans can be.'

'I used to be able to change the channel when stories about these kinds of people were on,' he continued. 'I now don't have the luxury to do that, and when I lost Noah, I woke up and realised that people who spread these stories are more interested in propagating fear than getting at the truth. And the human cost of that is phenomenal.' Pozner believes that only a few years ago countermeasures worked. Then the level of troll investiture became too high.

The president and his media enablers are working hard to pre-emptively discredit the Mueller investigation. Their accusations of bias, fishing expeditions and witch-hunts do not have to be credible or even coherent. They only have to present a posture, not a position, and this posture somehow becomes more effective as it shifts. Accountability can't seem to stick to something so slippery. The shared realities of the Watergate era were fractious, contingent and hypocritical. But even those tense truces no longer exist.

I took a walk through the Capitol Hill district in Washington the other day, past the Supreme Court and the Library of Congress, and thought how deceiving this Latinate vision of the past is. All the neoclassical architecture is supposed to represent, in articulate marble lines, a society run according to order and reason. But Rome was governed by superstition. It was a place where the fates of men rested on patterns in the flights of birds, spots on sacrificial livers, everything from fire in the sky to a sneeze. Welcome back.

ALT-RIGHT ON THE NIGHT

Does anyone admit to being a racist anymore? Online, even self-declared neo-Nazis insist they're not bigoted, and for a while I collected the most dissonant of these finds. There was the British man who visited his local Asda supermarket wearing a full SS uniform, and afterwards told the *Daily Mail* that he didn't 'hate anyone … it's not about the politics for me'. He added, 'I just live and breathe everything Adolf Hitler' – clearing up any misunderstanding. At the 2017 Unite the Right event in Charlottesville, Virginia, a twenty-year-old white supremacist named Peter Cvjetanovic was photographed amid the torch-bearing, screaming mob. He too was screaming and bearing a torch, but afterwards said to a Reno TV station that he was 'not the angry racist they see in that photo'. So who was he?

I felt prepared, then, for some of the awesome breaches in self-awareness at Unite the Right's sequel in Washington, but it was still surreal to stand in the D.C. drizzle and listen to white nationalists saying things like, 'I don't care what race you are!'

'To be honest, I'm not really a nationalist,' said one of the speakers onstage.

'We're even more diverse than they are!' said another, gesturing to the 3000 baying anti-racism protesters across Lafayette Square.

It was Walter Benjamin who thought the key to understanding fascism was its style, the elisions that could heroically unify impossible contradictions. Here was the 'aestheticisation of politics' he was writing about, expressing itself through extreme cognitive dissonance and tan chinos.

I had to queue twice to get into the event, and was luckier than some: one writer for an African-American website didn't even manage visual contact with the attendees. By then it was unclear what the actual event was. Was it the rally itself? Was it the sizeable counter-protest? Was it the media pack? The imbalance in the participants – thirty-one white nationalists, dozens of media, hundreds of police, thousands of counter-protesters – was so substantial that it seemed self-perpetuating, like the body-politic equivalent of an autoimmune disease.

Since the first Unite the Right had resulted in the killing of a counter-protester (it says a great deal about the racialisation of crime in America that this murder – caused by a neo-Nazi deliberately ramming a crowd with a car – is rarely called a terrorist act), the Peter Cvjetanovics of the world had found themselves pariahs, sometimes outcast from their own families. Unite the Right 2 was held on this inauspicious anniversary, a move too provocative even for semi-professional haters: both the prominent white nationalist Richard Spencer and the alt-right Stormfront Radio had advised supporters to stay away. Security was heavy. As a sniffer dog went over our bags, one cameraman said he felt as chaperoned as a preschooler on an excursion.

For me, the vibe was closer to a sideshow or a gimp exhibit:

unimpressed groups on rotation, ushered behind a barrier for mid-range glimpses at a disappointing horror. It didn't help that the rally was literally over before it began – despite a scheduled start time of five-thirty, police were vanning the attendees out by five – and this scanty and goonish gathering looked even more ridiculous than usual as they fronted clutches of TV cameras under a thunderstorm. The snipers on the White House roof added no gravity.

Perhaps this shit-show was a sign that the alt-right had faltered, that its white tide of resentment had receded, or that there was never really a tide at all, just a big puddle. Certainly organisers took it as a sign of failure. The consensus was that counter-protesters, especially antifa activists, had created a hostile enough environment to shrink the marches. These antifa were sometimes pushy with reporters, especially when filmed. One masked man rationalised this to a journalist after his phone was thrown across the street: 'It's historically inaccurate to say you can beat fascism peacefully.'

Anti-antifa rhetoric might be Unite the Right's most widespread legacy. It gave the right-wing media an opportunity to prove the brainstem-level idea that 'both sides do it' could still operate even in the face of genocidal wannabes. 'The idea that Nazis and people who oppose Nazis are somehow equatable is the most batshit fucking crazy shit I've ever fucking heard,' the actor Seth Rogen tweeted, a statement that already sounds like a time capsule from a saner point in time. Antifa groups are now routinely described as 'the real fascists' or 'just as bad as the Nazis'. New York congressman Peter King and his buddies introduced a bill called the 'Unmasking Antifa Act of 2018', which proposed fifteen-year jail terms for masked demonstrators caught committing felonies. The Irish-American King is also famous for his long-standing support for the Irish Republican Army. He once said that the fight against British imperialism was 'a dirty war on both sides'.

There seems to be no record of a murder committed by an antifa member; in contrast, the Southern Poverty Law Center, a non-profit legal advocacy organisation, found that members of just one white-nationalist online forum – Stormfront – committed almost 100 murders between 2009 and 2014. The best counterargument to white supremacy is still its adherents, and there in Lafayette Square were the dregs of the dregs. Like the fall of Berlin, all that was left were motley hold-outs: old men and young boys.

There were even some people of colour, more common than you might think at events like these. They wanted attention, or were there as a matter of principle taken to the absurd – an African-American man called Brandon Watson was attending to support the First Amendment. Perhaps mutually assured self-destructiveness – always underrated for its seductive powers – was creating some kind of solidarity. Walter Benjamin also wrote that humankind under modern media was so self-alienated that it could 'experience its own destruction as an aesthetic pleasure of the first order'. That sentiment has explanatory power for individuals as well as eras, including our own.

Television did seem more apposite than the Third Reich. Only a few weeks before Unite the Right 2, *The Jerry Springer Show* was cancelled, after 4000 episodes of what *TV Guide* called 'the worst show in the history of television'. You might remember that along with deadbeat husbands and teens who insisted on doing what they wanted, white-nationalist guests were a favourite folk villain for the daytime audience. Perhaps the program was cancelled only because it had been superseded. Its job was done.

On the ground, the menace of the first Unite the Right was gone, and in its place was something eerily reminiscent: magnets for loathing who clearly just wanted to get on TV, protected by security from a live crowd trying to hit them, all filmed for the pseudo-education of viewers at home. As I half-heartedly interviewed a computer programmer (of course) who wanted to sue YouTube, I couldn't shake the feeling I might inadvertently be acting more like a talk-show host than a reporter. Springer even had a name for the unique style of brouhaha he pioneered in this arena: a 'klanfrontation.'

As we trudged off, one anchor opened his umbrella and said, 'I felt like an asshole walking around with this thing all day, but it turns out I needed it.' It was a bit like that: insufficient countermeasures had allowed the first Unite the Right to occur, and diminished media antibodies had allowed more virulent strains of white nationalism to spread again. An overcorrection was better than no correction.

But if the city was not paralysed by the protest, it was at least stricken by it. The attendees had essentially been given police escorts, at the price of $2.6 million, but the real expense was the opportunity cost, the now-familiar feeling that the smartest people were all somehow stuck talking about the stupidest. The inability to distinguish between virulence and influence, the threat inflation that is fed by hate speech on the internet – there are no readily apparent solutions to these problems, and no sign of them diminishing, only changing form. For now, we are stuck with platitudes. So take care of yourself, and each other.

AN ENERGY EXCHANGE

The venue for the 1968 Democratic National Convention in Chicago looks abnormal in retrospect. The organisers eschewed the shoreside of Lake Michigan, and the architectural gigantism of downtown, instead lighting on the International Amphitheater, which sat right alongside the acre-wide pig pens and abattoirs of the Union Stockyards. It was so close that attendees could smell blood coming from the packinghouses, and hear the screams of stuck livestock. Such voluntary proximity to this unclean industry was already an anomaly by the 1960s, but in the years prior, the Stockyards had been an attraction in their own right. Tours culminated in specially built galleries overlooking the killing floor, a theatre where the 'butchery of the world' offered one of the most concentrated and intense spectacles of modernity.

The amphitheatre had hosted political conventions before, and yet, it seemed to be unlucky: every ticket assembled under its roof, apart from one featuring Richard Nixon, had gone on to lose. The 1968 Democrats were unlikely to break that curse. Lyndon Baines Johnson, his popularity destroyed by the

Vietnam War, had withdrawn from recontesting the presidency (although he fantasised about swooping into the convention by helicopter to secure the nomination), and his anti-war heir apparent, Robert F. Kennedy, had been assassinated only two months before. No one held the position of presumptive nominee of the Democratic Party. It would be settled by a contest of pro- and anti-war forces, represented by the candidates Hubert Humphrey and Eugene McCarthy. Tens of thousands of protesters in two distinct groupings would sharpen the question, while Chicago's Democratic mayor, Richard Daley, insisted on order. Attendees described the convention centre as a 'fortress'. Before its siege, the demonstrators threatened to put LSD in the city's water supply, a prank that in the already paranoid circumstances registered as a threat.

Even by the febrile standards of the period, history in the first half of 1968 was made in almost apocalyptic succession. World-changing occurrences were so close-set they overlapped: on 29 August, just as the tensions of the Chicago convention finally broke from skirmishes into an all-out riot, Czech newspapers were closing for a Soviet-ordained 'day of reflection'. It was the beginning of the end of the Prague Spring. Measured in memory against the Tet Offensive, which began in January, and the Paris uprising in May, Black Power shootouts and FBI assassinations, the convention feels less exceptional, and Chicago's memory might put more stock in the south- and west-side rioting after Martin Luther King Jr's assassination in April. There, the chaos was so concentrated that almost 600 fire alarms were triggered in one 24-hour period.

The Black Panther Billy 'Che' Brooks remembers the convention as the moment that police brutality was applied to

Caucasians for a change. While the Panther leader Bobby Seale spoke to the assembly, it did not much register in the 'neighbourhoods' (Seale was later charged for incitement, and at trial, the judge ordered him bound and gagged, slave-style). The columnist and broadcaster Rick Kogan, a Chicago institution, visited the demonstrations as a sixteen-year-old, wearing his father's World War II jacket. He went more to party than to protest, and only later, in more careful reflection, realised that he had embroidered his memory from press reports. At the time it had not felt so important after all. 'We were just part of a few really bad days and nights,' he wrote on the fiftieth anniversary.

The jubilee in 2018 was staid and reflective, and there were still detectable levels of shame, or some shame-adjacent emotion. A panel at the University of Chicago at Illinois, held fifty years to the day after the police rushed the crowds in Grant Park, took its title from the protesters' cry: 'The Whole World is Still Watching'. Marilyn Katz, a high-schooler and a Students for a Democratic Society organiser in 1968, outlined the mythology. 'We were active, then burned out and drugged out,' she said, but she maintained that organisers had played an enduring role changing society. That made the Battle of Michigan Avenue – in which protesters and police clashed, and police used brutal violence – catalytic, at least. Don Rose, formerly of the National Mobilization Committee to End the War in Vietnam, said the lesson was to 'stay out of the way of billy clubs', but in the question-and-answer session afterwards, where the mics quickly became monopolised by boomerish autobiography, the former hippies were sure to mention that they, too, had been beaten. One man described regaining consciousness, cradled by his father. There was some nostalgia for the draft – it had compelled levels of activism unrepeated since, and a political-science major noted that few students were in attendance. Starbucks provided the coffee.

At Grant Park itself, a youth dance company called Move Me Soul was 'reassembling' a well-known photo of the thronged protestors clustered around an equestrian statue. The monument, to the Union Army general John Logan, sits at the apex of a rise, at the end of a neat grassy plot that looks very much like a battlefield. It was not hard to see how it had become such contested terrain, or why the sight of hippies mounting a brass horse got the police so infuriated. The dancers, dressed as Panthers, each carried a placard depicting an individual cut out from the original photo. These images were blurred and blown up into psychedelic colour, and carried up the hill while a trumpet and a saxophone played an improvised dirge. The meagre audience then joined in to fill out the 'crowd'. It was mournful and inorganic, and the careful placards, mounted on clean pinewood, seemed only to confirm how the energy of the original gathering had been dispersed. There was an anniversary protest elsewhere, but it barely registered.

The real memorials were produced at the time of the event, in reports and films and photos. The televised version has since become almost a shorthand for the 1960s: grainy, sepia policemen, clubs swinging out of clouds of tear gas, bearded young men running, indistinct animal shapes – images that could just as easily have been taken in Birmingham, or Watts, or Newark, or Detroit, apart from the presence of white faces on the black-and-white film.

The convention's political significances might be debatable, but as a cultural happening, especially as a literary event, it was unparalleled and unrepeatable. The press corps in attendance was huge – almost one reporter for every two attendees – and filled with luminaries. *Esquire* decided to treat it as theatre-in-the-street, and sent William S. Burroughs, Jean Genet and Terry Southern (Samuel Beckett was too ill to attend, and something went wrong with Eugène Ionesco). They were wrangled by a young John Berendt, and reinforced by the war correspondent John Sack in case this A-team got too high to write. Their photographer was Michael Cooper, who took the sleeve shot for *Sgt. Pepper's Lonely Hearts Club Band,* though the pieces for the most part ran as uninterrupted text.

Norman Mailer was there reporting; so too Renata Adler, Studs Terkel and Jimmy Breslin. *The New York Review of Books* sent William Styron and Elizabeth Hardwick. Arthur Miller was inside at the convention; Allen Ginsberg and Ed Sanders were outside in the park. MC5 played for the protesters, Aretha Franklin sang for the conventioneers (her soul version of 'The Star-Spangled Banner' caused a racist microcontroversy). Bumming a joint, Hunter S. Thompson wrote what might have been the first true piece of gonzo journalism (it remained unpublished at the time). On television, Walter Cronkite and Dan Rather reported live, while Gore Vidal and William F. Buckley added acidic analysis. Their debate about the violence produced the iconic moment where Vidal called Buckley a crypto-Nazi, and Buckley responded by calling him a queer and threatening to punch him. There is, in this moment of reactionary cool becoming heat and hatred, a synecdoche for the whole event.

The list of Yippie demands mentioned art more often than war (and fucking more often still). Their gathering was intended, said one of their leaders, Abbie Hoffman, as 'a blend of technologists and poets, of artists and community organizers, of anyone who has a vision'. The effort was to 'develop a Community of Consciousness'. Anyone coming to Chicago, Hoffman said, 'should begin preparations for five days of energy-exchange ... The possibility of violence will be greatly reduced. There is no guarantee that it will be entirely eliminated. This is the United States, 1968, remember. If you are afraid of violence you shouldn't have crossed the border.'

The borders were so clear that they became straight dialectical clichés: right versus left, war versus peace (with the forces of peace pre-doomed), old versus young, hate versus love, policeman versus protester, establishment versus anti-establishment, nightsticks against rock music. At this bull-market moment in American masculine nonfiction, the writers were performers too, cast in the role of themselves, and the themes confronting them were similarly broad and irresistible. So the abattoirs provided a literal representation of the mechanised slaughter of Vietnam (as well as a porcine reference point for the police). William Styron watched protesters being beaten outside the window of the Conrad Hilton, as through a television screen, and as the glass shattered, he felt his pretence of objectivity go as well. When the police began to attack card-carrying reporters and camera operators, it was outrageous, but also confirmed their importance, and their self-importance. How could the press remain impartial while being physically attacked? The liberal media knew its purpose – to throw light on abuses of power. Here was the power. Here was its abuse.

The theatre had become a morality play, but its audience did not react as anticipated. When Hunter S. Thompson copped a baton in the solar plexus, he joked that it was the moment he decided to vote for Nixon. But those watching at home were not joking. An energy exchange had taken place, but instead of the kind intended, it was a counter-revolution. Letters poured in to newspapers supporting Daley and the police, blaming the protesters and the press, going so far as accusing them of staging the event. The most influential piece of writing came not from the all-that literary contingent, but from a workaday columnist, Joseph Kraft, who set out to describe the voters who sided with the billy clubs and came up with a new term: 'middle America'.

Twenty-eighth August 1968 may not have been exactly 'the night America decided to vote for Nixon', but something firmed and hardened then, and in its wash-up, the media began a self-examination, almost a self-flagellation, that never really stopped. The person who best understands this change, historian Rick Perlstein, lives in Chicago. The city is still one of the best vantage points to look back at America's turn to the right, which he has described in the books *Before the Storm*, *Nixonland* and *The Invisible Bridge*. Sitting in the offices of the magazine *In These Times,* he says the real importance of the convention came from the beating of the press. 'It was *the* galvanising event for this kind of guilt-soaked reckoning that the media didn't understand middle America. That they [middle America] sided with the police.'

'The press craves this crystalline moral theatre of violence being visited on innocents,' Perlstein continues. 'But the public's sympathies are with the police, provoked by the kids.' There is a direct line between that trauma and the press today 'interviewing every last Trump supporter in every last diner in every red state in America. That joke comes from somewhere: the idea that the true America is conservative, that it abhors protest and that somehow people who protest against wars are alien to heartland values.' When Nixon won, he positioned himself as a tribune of quiet against the party of clamour, and the quiet was reified in his most famous formulation, the 'silent majority'. The media also felt they had underestimated middle America's puritanism. This wasn't quite right – the resentment towards protesters was in part class-based (college students could defer the draft to Vietnam, whereas someone like, say, the brother of a police officer could not), but it was also a complex response to expressed sexuality, what Perlstein calls 'fugitive rage' about the 'fucking in the streets'. 'These psychological pas de deux – one of the reasons Old Hollywood and the people around Reagan despised the hippies so much was because they had this kind of monopoly on hedonism. And the hippies were democratising hedonism.' This was an acute threat in Chicago, a convention city where the hypocrisy around adultery-for-hire and business propriety was vital. (When John Steinbeck visits Chicago in *Travels with Charley,* he writes about a brief stay in a dirty room at the Ambassador East, where the prior occupant's female companion 'used a heavy perfume but did not stay the night'.)

Norman Mailer, someone too well acquainted with the confusions between desire and anger, understood the political component of this perfectly. The Yippies, he wrote:

> did not necessarily understand how much their simple presence hurt many good citizens in the secret velvet of the heart – the Hippies and probably the Yippies did not quite recognize the depth of that schizophrenia on which society is built. We call it hypocrisy, but it is schizophrenia, a modest ranch-house life with Draconian military adventures;

a land of equal opportunity where a white culture sits upon a Black ... a land of family, a land of illicit heat; a politics of principle, a politics of property ... What the Yippies did not recognize is that their demands for all-accelerated entrance into a twentieth-century Utopia ... was nonetheless equal to straight madness for the Average Good American, since his liberated expression might not be an outpouring of love, but the burning of his neighbor's barn. Or, since we are in Chicago, smashing a good neighbor's skull with a brick from his own back yard.

The protests, as Mailer put it, represented the 'destruction of every saving hypocrisy'.

Driving with Perlstein, we saw a Grateful Dead numberplate while considering a question: where did the energy behind the protests go? 'There's one of your answers,' he said. A jam band that travelled until the tie-dye faded. The hippies scattered, and those who stayed together tended to do so at concerts, not protests.

But did part of 'liberated expression' wind up in the Southernisation of the Midwest? The radicalism and liberalism of what was once called 'Prairie Power' are disappearing, in favour of out-of-state country music and Confederate flags.

'The Southernisation of America,' says Perlstein. 'My life's work.'

In the *Esquire* dispatches from the convention, there is a constant and malign zoological theme – not just the pigs, but apes and dogs and goats as well. Jean Genet began his piece, 'Chicago makes me think of an animal which, oddly, is trying to climb up onto itself', and William S. Burroughs finished his own idiosyncratic report by describing a scene in which a 'purple-assed mandrill' is elected president. The savage animal is then shot dead by a policeman, and 'thumps to the ground and bloody grass, he ejaculates, shits and dies'.

'I say to you that Grant Park will be a shrine to all future Americans,' Burroughs wrote, though fifty years on the shrine looks more like a monument to defeat. One that has been desecrated in the interim.

NOTES ON SOME ARTEFACTS

Five or six years ago, around the period most people seemed to be spending almost all of their time on the internet, I began to notice a particular kind of online phenomenon, for which I did not have a name. I started to call these moments 'artefacts', borrowing a word from photography that refers to the machine-created distortions and ghosts that corrupt digital imagery. 'An unintended alteration in data' is one definition, but this new kind of 'artefact' was expanding beyond sporadic instances and becoming a persistent glitch in the discourse at large.

The result was a type of semiotic collapse, one that found its fullest expression in the 2016 presidential campaign, when news stories fabricated in Macedonia gained a wider reach than *The Washington Post*. Countermeasures to interference in the 2018 congressional election looked ineffectual, perhaps deliberately so. Artefacts helped define the contest, and also featured in the confirmation process of the prospective Supreme Court Justice Brett Kavanaugh. During the hearings, footage was broadcast of Kavanaugh's former clerk, Zina Bash, sitting behind the nominee, making an 'OK' signal with one hand – thumb and forefinger forming a circle, the other three fingers splayed – while it rested on her opposite arm. This was interpreted as a secret sign, an insignia for 'white power', and criticised online.

Bash – an improbable neo-Nazi – is descended from Holocaust survivors on her father's side, and Mexicans on her mother's. Her husband declared the conspiracy repulsive, and *The Washington Post* and others traced the lineage of the outrage to a prank on the message board 4chan. (Fittingly, this origin story was disputed.) On 4chan, trolls set out to trick members of the anti-racist left, persuading them that the arrangement of the fingers in the 'OK' gesture represented the 'w' and 'p' in the phrase 'white power'. Some took the bait; others, such as the Anti-Defamation League, did not. Then real white-power advocates began to use the symbol themselves, so the 'fake' white-power symbol became a real one. When liberals objected, they were called hysterical and paranoid, imagining racism in innocuous gestures. When someone prominent throws an 'OK' in America, the illusion that they secretly support white power cannot be fully dispelled. So is it a real or unreal symbol of white supremacy? It is both, and neither. It has non-Newtonian properties. It is an artefact.

Like an obscenity, an artefact is easier to experience than to describe, though it can be triangulated. First, none of those participating in an artefact apprehend its full meaning. This creates a sinister and alienated sensation removed from human agency and intention. Take the Slovenian art rock band Laibach, who formed in 1980 when Slovenia was still communist, and adopted a fascistic and militaristic aesthetic as an ambiguous critique of state power. In 2015, Laibach became the first Western rock band to play in North Korea. This means that a totalitarian regime conspicuously eased its repression by scheduling a band that mimicked totalitarian regimes as protest against a different, now defunct totalitarian regime. Even Western audiences struggle to parse Laibach, let alone North Koreans, who had never seen music that was not state-sanctioned and were expected to decipher martial versions of Western pop songs they had never heard. Laibach played songs from *The Sound of Music*. The DPRK party paper called the concert 'very interesting and a success'.

Second, an artefact would have been impossible to explain to someone twenty years ago. In August 2014, the official Twitter account of Pope Francis offered up a prayer for the suffering: 'Lord, we pray that you sustain those who have been deprived of everything in Iraq. #prayforpeace'. It attracted a reply that attained notoriety: '@Pontifex DESTROY MY PUSSY WITH YOUR GIANT MONSTER COCK'. This tweet may have been the product of a bot, which means, unlike the scabrous anti-clerical smut of the French Enlightenment, it was a bloodless and unintentional blasphemy. Imagine trying to explain this to a visitor from the past. Who swore at the Pope? Probably a robot. Who built the robot? Nobody knows. How did the robot come to speak to the Pope? Anyone can speak to the Pope now. There were attempts to reason with the bot, as though it had violated its directives. 'Please have some respect. We are asking for prayers for the mass killing of innocent people!' one account replied.

The combination of international, rapid and multifarious online information exchange creates the conditions for artefacts. But it is the algorithmic currents driving the internet that sees them so ascendant. We do not know the effect of super-computers controlling human meta-desire, a situation that is under-appreciated. It barely draws comment, for example, that many humans in Western countries are engaged in a machine-directed, mildly eugenic breeding program thanks to online dating (already, two forms of relationships – those featuring significant height discrepancies, and those between childhood sweethearts – are far less common than they used to be). The effect of these algorithms on forming political persuasions and voter intentions already looks ominous, but the next generation will be incubated by them almost exclusively, just as the sophistication and pace of these programs begins to really insinuate itself into our collective political minds.

I admit that I was sceptical that computers, and nefarious people operating them, were able to sway the result of the 2016 presidential election. It seemed implausible that an event this complex could be altered by social-media posts full of obvious lies. If such crude disinformation (and so little of it, comparatively) could cripple America, the country must have been on its last legs already. I am now not so sure about this, because I think the mechanism of action might be elsewhere. It is not the posts that are effective – like any sort of internet post, they have negligible, marginal value. It is the accounts publishing the posts that have the impact, and they have a different purpose altogether.

Around one year ago, a journalist I know came across a standard pro-Trump trolling/bot account on Twitter. These are sometimes called 'MAGAhead' accounts, and their bio descriptions are flavoured with patriotic stock phrases. This account was named @GuntherEaglemann. 'Gunther' was said to be 'Fighting the good fight! #BackTheBlue and Support our Troops, USMC, Conservative | Helping the confused Left turn Right – one at a time'. His location was listed as Texas, USA, and he had 2335 followers. The journalist knew that Gunther Eaglemann did not exist because the picture of 'Gunther' was a picture of himself. Once challenged, the account disappeared.

Who was Gunther Eaglemann? Who was behind this doppelganger? Was he a human or a machine? On initial impression, the account was created to mimic an American conservative, and then bolster or signal boost conservative-aligned posts. His name is hyperreal, somehow more American than real American names, like a Darryl Archideld or a Bobson Dugnutt. But what if instead of a copy, Gunther is a template? What appear to be bot accounts have begun adorning themselves with even more unnatural symbolism, including emojis of flags, MAGA hashtags and Bible verses. Here is an example:

> Southern Belle ⚜ Cajun*Irish 🎭 🇺🇸 US Military 🇺🇸 & LEOs 🤍🇺🇸 🇺🇸 "Happy girls are the prettiest!" #MAGA 🇺🇸 Philippians 4:13 ✝

We can't say whether this is a bot account or if conservatives are modelling their online presences on bots. This seems to be especially true of older conservatives. It is not the disinformation that is memetic, it is this formulaic eyesore 'style', which some users seem to be mimicking wholesale, either as an act of solidarity, or as a piece of trolling, or because they have a fluid and uncertain political position driven by emotion, which then takes shape as a learned behaviour. Online audiences are experiencing artefacts. But they are also becoming them.

The technology writer James Bridle's essay 'Something Is Wrong on the Internet' resulted in a slew of children's content being banned from YouTube. Bridle wrote about a genre of videos where animators or specialist performers acted out themes and settings generated by algorithms, with often non-sensical and occasionally disturbing results. 'BURIED ALIVE Outdoor Playground Finger Family Song Nursery Rhymes Animation Education Learning Video' is a long way from *Sesame Street*. The real significance, he wrote, was the lack of intent: the human beings involved may not have intended any of these outcomes, and the exploitation and dehumanisation were instead predictable systemic outcomes.

You can start to sense the political implications of these insights. The transmission of conspiracy theories is much more rapid. Try making online enquiries about the Federal Reserve, vaccines, the September 11 attacks or the Jewish religion, and the results are innundated with paranoia. The offline implications are limitless and, so far, overwhelmingly negative. 'Yesterday on facebook I saw a lady call a man she knows in real life a "bot" because he criticized Rachel Maddow', posted the account @subtlerbutler. (That lady might be onto something.) The shooting of the gorilla Harambe was not an artefact, but it became one, when a grotesque, meaningless event acted as a projection screen for off-piste and angry discussions about racism, zoo design, parenting and media discourse, all of which had nothing to do with an ape being assassinated.

The former NBA star Dennis Rodman being sent to North Korea to 'assist' in the peninsula peace talks, his fare paid for by a cannabis-backed cryptocurrency. That's an artefact.

The Trump administration is an artefact.

IN THE BIG HOUSE

There must be some deep, hidden relationship between American politics and American football, though no one knows what it is. So far, no theory linking the Founding Fathers to men in spandex pants has been satisfactory, perhaps because gridiron is such an exotic creature that it's not really like anything else at all, not even any other sport (Canadian football doesn't count). It is more a study in abstraction than a game: over more than three hours of play time, the football itself might be in motion for only ten minutes, and most players present are not supposed to handle it – an offensive linesman might complete a successful career never having touched the ball. The crowd can extend this faffing-to-action ratio further still, to a full day, thanks to tailgating, so-named for the pre-game tradition of people eating food from the rear end of their cars. Taken together, these on- and off-field phenomena are not just the most popular sport in America, but the most popular *thing* in America. Experiencing it is experiencing American culture at a pharmaceutical grade.

Football's fanbase is so large and dedicated that it is both the most and third-most watched sport on US television (the second-most watched is baseball, which was already looking old-fashioned when it was supplanted sometime in the 1960s). The professional National Football League ranks first in viewership, but college football ranks third, and many purists prefer it (*Sports Illustrated* once claimed, 'For fans of fun, the choice is clear'). The varsity version also tells a story about American priorities – in most places, the highest-paid state employee is a college football coach, and eight of the ten biggest stadia on earth are purpose-built for college football.

The single largest operational arena on earth is May Day Stadium in Pyongyang (where 'multipurpose stadium' means alternating between those dancers with the coloured cards, and dissidents being executed). But the second-largest in existence is Michigan Stadium at the University of Michigan in Ann Arbor, Michigan, which is nicknamed 'The Big House', and has been filled with more than 100,000 Michigan fans watching the Michigan Wolverines for 281 consecutive games, stretching back to the 1970s.

All those 'Michigans' might give you some sense of what being there is like, where it is the branding and not the building that creates the most awesome sense of scale. My hosts were distant relatives, a couple named Jim and Lois, mad fans from Toledo, Ohio (Jim was a Michigan Marching Band alumnus), who had been going to The Big House for forty years. I quickly lost count of the items of Wolverines merchandise in their house, most of it embossed with a block letter 'M'. In the middle of the night, I stumbled to the guest bathroom, switched on a football-shaped night-light, and was greeted by a bar of soap striped in the team's blue and maize colours.

On the morning of the game, Jim's car (with Michigan vanity plates) was loaded with a Wolverines ice bucket; a mimosa dispenser in the shape of a football helmet; three flags; three tables; a sunshade; two tablecloths; a selection of cutlery, plates and cups; and two lawn flamingos, all on theme. I was gifted a T-shirt that read 'It's Great to be a Michigan Wolverine', and Jim emblazoned the car doors with Wolverines magnets before departure (I offered to help, but there was a special order).

I wondered if this level of festooning might be overkill. Compared to the rest of the tailgaters, it looked almost discreet. Jim and Lois's set-up did not include a satellite TV dome jutting from the top of their truck, for example, or a portable tiki bar, or a custom-made flag detailing how long the family had been tailgating for, or an airbrushed vehicle depicting scenes of Michigan triumph on every panel.

Kick-off was at 3.30 pm, but by 9.30 am, schools and parking lots and golf courses neighbouring the stadium were resplendent with blue and maize canopies, like a medieval tournament. There were bus-sized motorhomes and custom-built trailers, and special areas where parking alone cost $500. In the near distance, a huge 'M' on the side of the stadium – several storeys high – hung over it all. The Big House carries no advertising, except for advertising for itself, and instead, light planes drag banners for car dealerships across the sky.

There was time to take a tour of the university sports facilities. A lot of American state-funded infrastructure looks tired or decrepit these days, so this outcrop of blooming public largesse was a shock. Near the Olympic-standard softball ground there was an ice-hockey rink. The state-of-the-art indoor football field turned out to have a roof too shallow for punting, so they built a roomier duplicate right next door. There was a special field for the marching band, who are said to spend more time drilling than the football team itself, and we caught them practising their high-step. Each of these fields had an observation tower – this one for the band director – and Jim was not the only one to joke that it reminded him of a prison. We had passed three prisons en route, one introduced to the traffic by signs that said 'DO NOT PICK UP HITCHHIKERS', and this pre-echo made me think of the pat Amerikkka explanations for the origins of American football.

In this version, what links American football and American politics is violence, the kind that the historian Richard Slotkin called 'regeneration through violence'. Early gridiron was so barbarous that it was sometimes fatal, and in 1905 the college game produced what the *Chicago Tribune* called a 'death harvest', where nineteen players died in one season, including three on a single November day. Teddy Roosevelt himself designed rules to prevent the game being banned; football would be safe without being anodyne, and still physical enough to temper the kind of men who made up Roosevelt's Rough Rider divisions during the Spanish–American War. It was as though the United States had become an heir to the Mesoamerican blood cults, making human sacrifices on the prairies instead of on holy ziggurats, with football somehow linked to the rites, just as the ancient Mayan 'ballgame' was.

Since September 11, there has been a real military element to the game too, over and above the metaphorical thread. When the band took to the field, this time in brass-buttoned uniforms, they marched in an M-shaped formation to the tempo of a drum major. They started with the University of Michigan's fight song

'The Victors' and finished with 'The Star-Spangled Banner'. As the
national anthem concluded, two F-35 Lightnings streaked low
over The Big House in a flyover. (These extravaganzas can cost
hundreds of thousands of dollars each, written off by the Air
Force or Navy as a recruiting tool.) This 'appreciation of military service' is omnipresent in American sport, and part of why
National Football League players protesting during the national
anthem attract such controversy. 'Dishonouring the troops' at a
football game constitutes secular sacrilege. Only one African-
American player, from the opposing Southern Methodist
University team, raised his fist, but it was a gesture so small and
peripheral that a sports reporter sitting next to me thought he
must be holding up a phone to take photos.

The protest did at least work as a reminder that viewing
American football solely as a proxy for militarism is a mistake.
It's too big and complex to be so smugly reduced. Michigan
versus SMU was not billed to be a classic (the visitors were
35-point underdogs with a leaky defensive), and it did prove
lopsided, though not as one-sided as the True Blue fans would
have liked. Still, it was enthralling for the initiated. Gridiron
is an acquired taste, and not a sport that is easy to understand
intuitively (half-watched on television, it matches Bill Hicks's
description of soft-core motel pornography – 'bobbing man-ass').
It is also an American-originated art form, like jazz or studio cin-
ema, and as creative a spectacle as either.

American football's depth means it repays dedication like
no other sport, perhaps why its fans are so invested. The most
jockish enforcer on a team still needs the intelligence to mem-
orise and reproduce hundreds of plays, while coaches rely on
whole encyclopaedias of theory and enterprise. This tactical

chess game is not rigid though, and so SMU committed to no huddle snaps, relying on uncalled and unplanned plays that tried to harness their athleticism, while papering over their deficiencies. Although it didn't work, their spontaneous and ingenious quarterback was so good to watch that it made you hopeful.

In the arena, the all-in patriotism and 'rooting' feels endearing and communal rather than fascistic. A same-sex couple, old friends of Jim and Lois, had joined our tailgate, and for them this unity of purpose was apparently linked to the upcoming elections in some unseeable way, as though America's true 'fan base' was rising up to best a rival. The Midwest was one of the key battlegrounds in the vote, and while Ann Arbor was liberal, it was possible to parse other cities and neighbourhoods almost street by street.

'It's like they're brainwashed,' said one half of the couple. 'Even my family. They have Fox News on twelve hours a day. I end my calls home by saying, "Mom, change the channel. I love you, but change the channel."' The 'M', she said, should stand for Mueller – 'Now there's a true patriot.'

The half-time show chimed with this. One of the more nationally humiliating moments of my life was enduring an Australian Football League Grand Final half-time show alongside a visiting American. As he watched Thirsty Merc or some other forgettable three-piece jam on a shabby riser, the signs of cognitive dissonance flooded over his face, as though he'd ordered dinner in a restaurant and been served a single pea. It couldn't have been more different in The Big House. The theme of the half-time show was the importance of voting, and the band formation spelled out 'We the People' in perfect copperplate, before morphing into turnout statistics. Only 55 to 60 per cent of those eligible to vote do so, the marching band semaphored, while big-screen broadcast quotes from John McCain and Barack Obama garnered applause. It should have looked ridiculous. But soundtracked by the thunder of the drumline, and in the very same venue where LBJ had first announced the Great Society platform, it instead felt unironically majestic.

THE DEVIL'S TRIANGLE

Plane passengers watched their headrest TVs and cried. The phones on Wall Street went unanswered for a time. On 27 September, in coffee shops and bars and in their homes, Americans united to watch what they knew would be a piece of history, live and televised. The United States Senate Committee on the Judiciary hearing received testimony from two people: Brett Kavanaugh, a federal judge nominated to the Supreme Court, and Dr Christine Blasey Ford, a psychology professor who said that Kavanaugh had sexually assaulted her thirty-six years ago, when they were both in high school. The testimony lasted all day, and by the end of the hearing, it was clear that the outcome, whatever it would be, would be unacceptable to half the country.

Very few social movements have created such rapid cultural change as the #MeToo campaign to call out sexual assault. 'Christine Blasey Ford Finds Herself at the Center of America's #MeToo Reckoning', CNN claimed, and while the movement might have spurred on the allegations themselves, the investigative mechanisms to hear them are yet to catch up. There might be no good judicial or executive body yet in existence that can determine the truth of a historical sexual assault. But it's hard to think of one less well suited than the committee, which, despite its name, is a near-guaranteed venue for travesties of justice.

Ford was testifying to eleven Republicans and ten Democrats (the Republicans were all white men, and the only minority represented among them was Mormons). Together, these committee members created a Frankenstein's monster: the prosecutor from court proceedings, but applied solely to the plaintiff, grandstanding interruptions from the panel, and opportunities to admonish and commiserate, sometimes at the same time, all sectioned into five-minute blocks. The chairman, Senator Chuck Grassley, assiduously watched the clock. He tried to project concern for Ford, but what seeped through was his concern for the confirmation vote that Friday.

Grassley's demeanour was part of a wider effort at Republican restraint, a kernel of self-awareness that eleven sour-faced old men interrogating a crying accuser might look sexist (this attempt at best behaviour still cracked – Senator Orrin Hatch told reporters that Ford was an 'attractive witness', and when asked to elaborate, said 'she's pleasing'.) The avuncular mode was almost worse than outright chauvinism, a festival of concern-trolling conducted through an appointed female representative, an Arizona prosecutor called Rachel Mitchell. Mitchell explored the uncomfortable tactic of trying to console and discredit Ford at the same time.

Ford was so forthright and credible that no one dared to question whether she had been assaulted. Instead, the questioning was laced with a pernicious idea: it was a case of mistaken identity. This balloon had been floated already, and had not gone well on its maiden voyage. Ed Whelan, a former deputy assistant attorney-general during the George W. Bush years, had claimed on Twitter that another man was responsible, proffered floor plans as evidence, implicated someone innocent, and then apologised and prepared himself for a lawsuit. But now the Mystery Man theory was back, and on social media conservative commentators suddenly embraced a century's worth of defence lawyer ambit claims. Eyewitnesses make mistakes. The human memory is fallible. Perhaps that's why we never learn anything.

Ford's expertise meant that she was able to speak to the brain chemistry of memory herself. The sole eyewitness, a former frat boy called Mark Judge, was holed up in a beach house in Delaware. Why he was not compelled to give testimony was never satisfactorily explained. Instead, Mitchell cycled through gentle, insinuating queries, which never quite became lines of questioning. Who had paid for the polygraph? Was it true she was afraid of flying? The White House was said to be displeased with these tactics, but the fix was already in. President Trump began calling senators mid-testimony, firming up their votes, growing impatient with the show trial's lack of finale. Scrutiny was applied to Republican moderates – politicans such as Susan Collins, Jeff Flake, Lisa Murkowski and Ben Sasse – who could each end the nomination with a vote. They had not stopped anything significant so far.

There was a lot of talk about the burden of proof. Should it be beyond reasonable doubt? A preponderance of evidence? Clear and convincing evidence? The trouble with a pseudo court is that no one knows the process. But everyone knew the Rule: the man usually wins, doubly so if they're a man like Brett Kavanaugh.

The Clarence Thomas hearing in 1991 had already put a credibly accused sexual harasser onto the court (two of the members of the current committee – Grassley and Hatch – had voted for Thomas). Kavanaugh had assisted in the cross-examination of Bill Clinton, and was extra keen that counsel ask the president if he had ejaculated in Monica Lewinsky's mouth. But the true low watermark was set, as always, by Donald Trump.

Was the committee considering accusations of twenty sexual assaults? Had the accused confessed to them on tape? Whatever came out, Republican base voters had already decided it could be lived with, or even embraced. An NPR/*PBS NewsHour*/Marist poll found that 54 per cent of Republicans believed Kavanaugh should be confirmed to the Supreme Court *even if Ford's allegation of sexual assault was found to be true*. When Kavanaugh began his statement, sometimes crying, sometimes yelling, so angry the pages snapped when he turned them, he was defending not just himself, but a whole system of entitlement and immunity that had already been found culpable – and survived. 'Judge Kavanaugh showed America exactly why I nominated him,' Trump tweeted afterwards. Too right.

Every Republican senator began their remarks by apologising to Kavanaugh, a perverse display of what the philosopher Kate Manne calls 'himpathy'. Of course Republican senators acted in bad faith and grandstanded – that's the job – but the wider trends in the conservative movement were less expected. There had been centre-right ambivalence about Kavanaugh – the Republican Senate Majority Leader Mitch McConnell had warned Trump against his nomination – but, counterintuitively, that vacillation ceased in the face of the accusations. It was the moment many 'Never Trump' conservatives came home. For example, the former *RedState* writer Erick Erickson, driven into the wilderness after a crisis of faith about Trump's character, tweeted in Kavanaugh's favour more than 250 times in a 24-hour period. These men appealed to psychology, graphology and sometimes theology to persuade themselves, but all the evidence they really needed was an 'honourable' career-conservative legal eagle under attack. This was a step too far.

Senator Lindsey Graham suggested that in future, Republicans might make false allegations against Democratic nominees to even the score. It was described as the end for illusions of media bias, for respect for the rule of law, for the pretence of unbiased judicial nominations and nominees.

Jeff Flake let it be known that he would not vote for Kavanaugh unless the FBI conducted a further investigation. They were given one week, and at the end of it, could find no evidence to corroborate Dr Ford's testimony. There was no time to look very hard. After his nomination was confirmed, Kavanaugh's first public appearance was at the conservative Federalist Society, where he was given a standing ovation. The same month, Dr Ford revealed that she had already moved house four times due to death threats.

HEAVY WATER

The seeds of cities are waterborne. Towns tend to germinate on harbours, streams, river mouths and flood plains, and most of the megalopolises of the future will retain these humble elemental foundations. Water is the thing that makes people live where they do (half the world's population takes sustenance from the watershed of the Tibetan Plateau alone). Perhaps that is why the city of Flint, Michigan, has become so internationally notorious. As the place with the poisoned water, it betrays what a city is for.

'Is Flint habitable anymore?' the MSNBC host Rachel Maddow asked, and some Flint residents objected, wondering what the question meant about their own vital condition. '"Is Flint viable?" would be a better question,' one Flintite said to me. I was with a small coterie of retirees, reporters and editors, and a sometime radio host, overlooking the black steel arches of Saginaw Street, one of the first places in America to be lit with electricity.

An hour's drive north-west of Detroit, Flint was founded on the Flint River, near Lake Huron. It operated first as a lumber town, then as a centre for car manufacturing. 'America is a thousand Flints,' Carl Crow wrote in 1945, when he was the Buick car-company historian, foretelling an apparent future illuminated by beacons like the Vehicle City. America is again a thousand Flints, only this time they describe a decline, what looks like the end of viability. Ass-kicked post-industrial wastelands; company towns minus the company. 'Shrinking cities' is one preferred term, places where the talent and initiative is siphoned away, and the primary industry left behind is trauma production, and vestiges of a few others: medical care, vice; a trickle of journalists and activists practising concern tourism.

Flint sits at a junction of dysfunction with a single cause: General Motors employed most of its residents, and then it stopped employing them. After decades of taking clean water from Lake Huron, corrupt bureaucrats instead chose to pipe their supply from the polluted Flint River, as a cost-saving measure. The water was not treated properly, and so it corroded lead pipes, becoming contaminated in the process. An unknown number of children will have developmental consequences as a result. There were outbreaks of legionnaires' disease, and twelve people died. There was a shoddy attempt at a cover-up, and Michigan's Republican governor, Rick Snyder, made mendacious claims that everything was fine. Four years later, it is still not fine.

Perhaps most lasting were the psychological miseries for Flintites. Back in Detroit, historian Anna Clark, author of *The Poisoned City*, had told me that the water crisis felt 'apocalyptic' for people in the community. 'Even for those who had endured a number of other indignities living in that city over the last many decades,' she said. 'They'd learned to be sceptical and grudgingly patient with things that are slower or not of the standard that they should be.' The water 'being damaged', as she phrased it, had made people reach for the language of Biblical plague, or genocide. 'Other life-and-death issues that can be related to those same decades of disinvestment in Flint – water still has a connotation they don't. It feels mythic, of mythic importance. Without it we die, and quickly.'

'There are two sources of lead here: the water and the bullets,' one rueful local joked, and those decades of disinvestment have left the city's trophy cabinet full of wooden spoons. If a year concludes without Flint judged the poorest or most dangerous city in America, it is usually a podium finisher. When the city is represented in the media, which is often (it is the centrepiece of Michael Moore's latest documentary, *Fahrenheit 11/9,* for example), it is as a warning. A routine and well-warranted complaint is that its human stories go unshown, that its population is caricatured or victimised. Only their 'resilience' is showcased, as though it is a chronic disease.

Part of the exasperation comes from stagnation: these reports don't change anything. At the turn of the twentieth century, the proliferation of photography helped end child-labour practices; fifty years ago, televised atrocities sapped public support for the Vietnam War. In the meantime, some link has gone missing between representation, humiliation and action. The media have always been voyeuristic, and the deal used to be that the voyeurism would result in action. Instead, the economy of attention hyper-inflated until it crashed, and only the voyeurism is left. The coverage of Flint is exhaustive to the point it is almost extractive. It becomes award-winning, then multi-award-winning, until … nothing happens.

The Midwestern United States is now the world centre for the Ballardian phenomenon of 'ruin porn'. In Detroit, abandoned buildings, the necrotic Gilded Age mansions of what used to be called 'the Paris of the West', are constantly molested by film students and art majors making chiaroscuro images of decrepitude, residents be damned. It's not just the amateurs who are at it, either: in the acclaimed (of course) documentary series *Flint Town,* one of the most disturbing scenes stars a ratty apartment succumbing to arson. It wasn't the fire that was unnerving, it was the shot: a cinematic overhead in crisp HD, taken from a drone that made the silent flames beautiful. 'We could have kept shooting, as Flint really never stops,' co-director Zackary Canepari told the website Creative Planet Network.

When flying cameras come to a place without potable water, you can sense the tension in what the Detroit reporter Thomas Morton called 'having your hometown overrun by a bunch of smug assholes with their reductive analogies' (the most documented 'faulty visual metaphors' in Detroit have nothing to do with the city's bankruptcy, and have been closed for many years). It takes a novel strain of inhumane abstraction to travel somewhere as apocalyptic as 7 Mile in Detroit, or Martin Luther King Avenue in north Flint ('it feels like a very long two miles,' one local said), and register these tragedies as pages in a coffee-table book.

There's not much value in adding a catalogue to the ruin-porn exhibition, even if it has the saving hypocrisy of hand-wringing. Flint can speak for itself. Treasure Hernandez, the 'urban' novelist who began writing her series of books set in the city while she was still in jail, calls it a 'dead city', 'a city where dreams are lost', 'literally a war zone'. 'Most of the people who lived there were poor, and not because they wanted to be,' she writes in *Choosing Sides.* 'But because it was the only way to be. Because of its ruthless atmosphere, the city produced some of the grimiest dudes, the sheistiest females, the most strategic hustlers, the baddest bitches and the most talented authors. Whatever the person's game was, they were usually the best at it because survival depended on it.' That's her description of resilience, one a less talented author can't better.

I would be tempted to bear witness to Flint silently, seeing that the calls for action are loud enough already, except there is a facet of the city I have not seen mentioned anywhere, one noteworthy enough to record. In all that poverty smut, there's never a mention of Flint's two small university campuses, its medical school, its international airport or its farmers' market. Downtown, or in the better suburbs, it could be anywhere in middle America, until it isn't. The singular image that haunted me afterwards was not shuttered factories or aimless citizens, but the Swartz Creek Municipal, a creek-side golf course, with a well-reviewed nine-hole executive option. A fifteen-minute walk from its fairways, an 87-year-old woman was robbed and raped at noon, and it is this closeness between the good and the bad, that same little distance you see between a hacienda and a favela, that so starkly demonstrates what Edgar B. Holt, of the National Association for the Advancement of Colored People's Flint chapter, called the 'magic lines for racial discrimination'.

The dirtiest secret of the worst city in America is that much of it is quite nice. Take Riverbank Park, continuous with the biggest of the campuses, the University of Michigan–Flint. It is a Lawrence Halprin–designed modernist concrete labyrinth, where the strolling lunchtime students look like they're auditioning for a pastel-drawn artist's impression. Birds dive in the river, and fat carp sit on the stones at the shallow base of a cascade. One minute's drive away, just across a bridge, is the start of north Flint, among the most dangerous neighbourhoods in America, a lattice of streets that could be in another country, not one enjoying good diplomatic relations with its neighbour. That border, created by the river, is a division between safe and unsafe, pleasant and unpleasant, comfortable and poor. No one much 'crosses over', and not just because of the smattering of security guards standing sentry.

North Flint was hard to look at, but it was even harder to see, and, except as a no-go area, it seemed to occupy little space in the consciousness of white Flint. 'I have much felt that so many whites have never seen any black ghettos,' the lay theologian William Stringfellow wrote in 1970. 'It is an almost incomprehensible blindness which afflicts most American whites ... they have not turned the corners or glanced away from their highways or crossed the tracks to see the black ghetto adjacent to their own lily-white ghetto.' The effect this had on whites, Stringfellow said, was that 'they do not realise that they are captives, and, hence, can they exist in a profound moral confusion, entertaining their own captivity as if it were their freedom'. There had been progress since – the white Flintites I spoke with knew they were confined in this way. Only they had no idea how to get out.

'You must read *Demolition Means Progress*,' one retired reporter told me, to general consensus that it 'explained it'. In this book, subtitled *Flint, Michigan, and the Fate of the American Metropolis*, historian Andrew R. Highsmith documents the pervasive power of Jim Crow in Flint, decades of prejudice expressed through employment, schooling, housing, loans, real estate practices, zoning, charitable foundations, churches, infrastructure, politicking, policing, and frank violence and intimidation. Segregation soaks the city down to the raw material used to

build it, a current as powerful as the river's. Until 1964, the par-
titioning continued post-mortem: almost all the cemeteries in
the region were covered by restrictive burial covenants that kept
white and black separated, past the point where those bodies had
skin. 'Ironically,' the author notes, 'this occurred during an era in
which northern cities such as Flint enjoyed strong reputations
for racial progressivism.'

Northern hypocrisy could, in its own way, be worse than
Southern bigotry. Those projects to 'overcome' segregation
instead enhanced it. By the late 1970s, Olive Beasley, sometimes
called the matriarch of the civil rights movement in Flint, saw that
a sluggish but ambitious program of urban renewal was really a
policy of 'Negro removal', as she put it. Tolerance flourished in the
abstract and died in the specific. In 1973, when the black home-
maker Rosaline Brown moved her family to the nearly all-white
Manley Village, she wanted to raise her children in an interracial
setting. 'I felt that the only way to improve this world is to get to
know people as persons,' she said. Two years later, twenty of her
twenty-four white neighbours had sold their houses.

Some shifted cities, others moved to white-flight satellite
townships that still exist. One, on the outskirts of Flint, sees
the per-capita average income almost double down a six-mile
stretch of road. The place is called Grand Blanc, in case you
missed the point. This is not subtle, and works in tandem with
a wider American tendency to build new things instead of
repairing old things (ideally, the new version can be resegre-
gated). In 1958, executives proposed founding a whole fresh
city called 'New Flint' almost next to the old one, as a de-facto
Caucasian duplicate where the car plants could be corralled.
Some in the city were happy to collude in its impoverishment,

enamoured of a decentralised model of living referred to as 'sub-urban capitalism'.

There are still pockets of prosperity in the city proper – what realtors call the 'college and cultural precinct' (how's that for prospective buyer flypaper?) has a row of Tudor-style mansions, with stucco colonnades and too-big lawns. They made me think of the British English slang term 'fuck-off houses', and help answer the question 'why would anyone want to live here?' The *National Review* writer Kevin D. Williamson, visiting Owsley, Kentucky, then the poorest county in the nation (it is now only the third poorest), noticed that 'for the smart and enterprising people left behind, life can be very comfortable, with family close, a low cost of living, beautiful scenery, and a very short climb to the top of the social pecking order. The relative ease of life for the well-off and connected here makes it easy to overlook the real unpleasant facts of economic life.' He too noted a golf course in what he called 'the Big White Ghetto', but 'so little in the way of everyday necessities'.

You do not have to be rich to live in a big house in Flint – a seven-bedroom home on Woodlawn Park Drive can be bought for US$249,000 – and the 'college and cultural set' do what they can. Still, I was taken aback the first time someone said, 'Phil Shaltz is one of our billionaires.' *One of?* Perhaps it is not the responsibility of these Phillionaires, as they are known, to fill the holes left by the absent state. Still, along with the charitable Mott Foundation (once a powerful force for the colour line), they have tried to spruce up downtown, refurbishing the theatre, making space for some pop-up stores, applying the 'creativity first' models that are supposed to have added ballast to other teetering cities. Shaltz's eccentric interventions focus on a campaign called 'I'm Concerned About The Blueberries', which began with a cryptic purple billboard bearing those words. It has not become much clearer since.

The Blueberry Ambassadorship for school-aged kids is 'a reminder to all of us to care about others' challenges – whether they seem monumental or perhaps as small as a blueberry'. It was inspired by a throwaway comment from a ski instructor, and for four years in a row Phillionaire Shaltz has thrown a party with pizza for the ambassadors. Sometimes he dresses as a giant blueberry. In the downtown, Shaltz also opened a New York–themed artisanal cocktail bar called X, where, he told the local news outlet *The HUB,* it takes eighteen minutes to make a drink 'the way we want to make it'. 'Stepping through the door of X, Flint native and developer Phil Shaltz's newly opened downtown lounge, is a bit like time travel,' *The HUB* cooed. Set the coordinates for the court of Marie Antoinette.

The sheer inessentialness of this emboldened me to ask the critical question out loud: 'Why does America so often mistake financial problems for moral problems?' Jan Worth-Nelson, the editor of the local *East Village Magazine,* blamed the Puritans. 'I come from that strain of American history. My people, my ancestors who came over, not on the *Mayflower,* but that kind of gang. I always feel like we struggled with this whole Protestant notion of individual salvation. Like it's the individual who is responsible to get right with God. And if you don't, you're a sinner. It's your own fault. That even gets translated into the sort of conflict you've always had between the collective and the individual, that we don't resolve very well.'

'You'll like Flint,' Anna Clark had told me, and I did like Flint. It had promise, after all. But I heard that after fifty years of unfulfilment, you can stop believing in promise. It wasn't just parochialism or delusion that kept these people here. They were fighting for something, or against something, and the sensation of malevolent intent behind their circumstances wasn't just a persecution complex. Perhaps not deliberate 'ethnic cleansing', as Michael Moore had called it. Palliative negligence? Cut losses? It was as though the city was on a do-not-resuscitate order. Power saw Flint as a sunk-cost fallacy.

Socialism and technology were discussed as solutions. Worth-Nelson's partner, Ted Nelson, thought that automation would lead to a universal basic income, fulfilling the spirit of 1968, back when he was an activist being beaten on the street.

But the technology was already here – Phil Shaltz is in the automation business – and the problems were not technical ones. Authorities almost went out of their way to prove this. They kept sending in the cavalry, only to have them shit in the street. When the Flint river water started to corrode car parts in the General Motors factory, GM's hydration source was switched back to Lake Huron. Naturally, the city kept drinking the rest. In June 2015 the US army arrived in town, not with engineers to fix the pipes, but to conduct exercises in 'the ability to (operate) in urban environments', rattling the east side with attack helicopters and midnight explosions. This show was widely received as a taste of what to expect if there was urban unrest.

Lacking was not only the will to place technology in the service of justice, but also the belief that this was a job for the government. States have delivered drinking water to their citizens for thousands of years, so this new inability means the anti-government manias of the United States have stripped some places back almost to the state of nature. 'It wasn't an act of

God,' said Clark. 'Not even in a climate-change-influenced way. It wasn't a private company that discarded all its pollution, and now we have to deal with it. These are the familiar templates that we have for dealing with environmental disaster. This one was man-made by the public sector, by the very departments that are meant to protect us against unsafe drinking water and all these other things.'

It was, she said, 'a test of how little government can do in an urban centre and get away with it. They pushed it to the limit. "How casually can we treat the wellbeing of these people? How little can we do for them before anybody else cares?"'

Sometimes the infrastructure ruin in Flint feels like the abandoned husk of another civilisation – like Dark Ages Italy marvelling at dry Roman aqueducts, but unable to make them flow. This is true of more humble buildings as well, and I wonder if these fallen middle-class neighbourhoods are less hopeful than slums, which at least have a chance of improvement and redemption, instead of the ever-present humiliation of what was.

Flint in its present condition is 55 per cent black, and leaving it, I could not shake the feeling that the city was like a purpose-built machine, fulfilling the same function it'd had all along, all the way to the point of self-destruction. Financially, it was being stripped for parts. You could imagine a sociopathic classical liberal argument that the provision of clean water to an economically unviable city was a moral hazard, the same way economists sometimes describe disaster relief as a moral hazard. A disaster of negligence was, in this view, an efficiency – a manifestation of what has at different times been called, with varying degrees of literalness, the whip hand. I was not sure that I liked Flint after all.

TRUTH KICKS THE BUCKET

Where were you when you heard that truth was dead? I must admit I've forgotten. Was it during George W. Bush's first term? Or maybe earlier, when Bill Clinton said, under oath, that it depended what the meaning of the word 'is' was. I do remember that by the mid-2000s liberals had decided a plastic Thanksgiving turkey was the perfect symbol of the Bush presidency (the fact that the fake turkey turned out to be real only made it more apposite). Not long after, a shell-shocked Al Gore wrote a book called *The Assault on Reason*. Perhaps it was Rush Limbaugh, or the internet, or the decline of teaching civics, but sometime between the World Book Encyclopedia era and the Wikipedia era, factual reality in America went out of whack and never went back.

This concern prompted *The New York Times*'s former chief book critic, Michiko Kakutani, to try authorship for the first time. Perhaps too slim to be called her 'first full-length book', *The Death of Truth* is at any rate her first half-length book, instigated by a sensation of 'losing a sense of shared reality and the ability to communicate across social and sectarian lines'. Her mission is to 'examine how a disregard for facts, the displacement of reason by emotion, and the corrosion of language are diminishing the very value of truth, and what that means for America and the world'. The battle-weary squad of George Orwell, Hannah Arendt, W.B. Yeats's 'The Second Coming' and Richard Hofstadter's essay 'The Paranoid Style in American Politics' are all called on for another tour of duty.

Kakutani is big on Orwell's 'prescience' in *Nineteen Eighty-Four* and the essay 'Politics and the English Language'. She is not the only one. These pieces of writing must surely rank as the most widely referenced political texts of the twentieth century, influential to the point of perniciousness. As Louis Menand has pointed out, if everyone from 'ex-Communists, Socialists, left-wing anarchists, right-wing libertarians, liberals, conservatives, doves, hawks, the *Partisan Review* editorial board, and the John Birch Society' can lay claim to Orwell's legacy, then perhaps some of his explanatory power is limited or vague.

Orwell is, I think, especially un-prescient about Trump. The authority in *Nineteen Eighty-Four* is sexless, socialist, parsimonious and bureaucratic, while Trump is promiscuous, mercantile, exuberant and vernacular. When he generates untruths prolifically, they come from boastfulness and ignorance more than from Machiavellian scheming – Big Brother wasn't watching morning telescreen shows and then railing to his aides about Goldstein. It's hard to think of a less Orwellian statement about America's history of violence than 'You think our country's so innocent?', but this vulgar restatement of plain fact in plain language does not improve the situation.

The idea that corrupt language creates corrupt politics wasn't invented by Orwell: Edward Gibbon, for example, thought that bad Latin grammar contributed to the fall of the Roman Empire. Like many aesthetically appealing ideas, it feels intuitively correct, but beyond the harmony is less convincing. It's unpersuasive in the aftermath of High Obamaism. Even allowing for the amnesiac nature of American political culture, it's astonishing how quickly liberals have erased the lessons of the post-Bush years, when all the civil centrism, conciliation and PG-13 rhetorical style they dream of was actually enacted – and spat back in their faces.

For Kakutani and her ilk, this repudiation is only temporary, one turn in a dialectical ballet. No one can pretend America was always rational; instead, the thinking goes, it has Apollonian and Dionysian periods (or fluctuations of superego and id, you can take your pick). There are bouts of popular excitement when reason goes to the canvas, science is ignored, experts are repudiated, idiots rise etc., we're just living through a particularly bad one. 'The Paranoid Style in American Politics' is offered as a guide to this tendency, but incautiously, as Hofstadter's essay outlines a very different dichotomy. Three of the paranoiacs it cites most prominently in the essay are the inventor Samuel Morse, the eminent scientist John Robison, and Lyman Beecher, the father of Harriet Beecher Stowe. It wasn't rubes advancing the conspiracies. It was 'rationalists'.

The trouble with *The Death of Truth*'s theory of politics is that it doesn't allow for the high folly of high minds. When titles like *The Best and the Brightest* and *The Smartest Guys in the Room* denote elite failure – and an elite failure that stretches from Vietnam to Iraq to Wall Street to the penurious condition

of the flyover states – the upper echelons should at least concede
that they are part of the problem. This doesn't stop them propos-
ing antidotes in the wrong places, though. Kakutani notes that

> liberals and conservatives, worried about the rise of nativ-
> ism and the politics of prejudice, warned that democratic
> institutions were coming under growing threat. Yeats'
> poem 'The Second Coming' ... experienced a huge revival
> in 2016 – quoted, in news articles, more in the first half of
> that year than it had been in three decades as commenta-
> tors of all political persuasions invoked its famous lines:
> 'Things fall apart; the centre cannot hold; / Mere anarchy
> is loosed upon the world.'

Like *Nineteen Eighty-Four,* 'The Second Coming' can only be
invoked so frequently if it is misunderstood. It is not a warning
about the 'danger flags' of fascism at all, but a totalitarian-curious
piece of pageantry *for* fascism, from a self-declared aristocratic
fascist. While Orwell was fighting with anarchists in the Spanish
Civil War, Yeats was writing marching songs for the other side –
he was one of the people Orwell was talking about when he
said, 'I believe also that totalitarian ideas have taken root in the
minds of intellectuals everywhere.' This symbiosis is now less
common, but still one the Apollonians have no real explanation
for. Why should we 'heed' this warning, if it didn't even work
on its author?

Fears about the death of truth are not dissimilar to Yeatsian
laments for the diminishment of high culture, and spring from
some of the same anxieties about the unwashed. This nostalgia for pipe-type intellectuals explains why a particular brand

of liberal critic blames postmodernism for Trump: even if he has 'never plowed through the works of Derrida, Baudrillard or Lyotard … some dumbed down corollaries of their thinking have seeped into popular culture and been hijacked by the president's defenders, who want to use their relativistic arguments to excuse his lies, and by right-wingers who want to question evolution or deny the reality of climate change', writes Kakutani. This is, to put it bluntly, not true.

It is an argument she has been running on various issues since at least 1993, and it has not become any more convincing in the meantime. It is least persuasive when applied to intelligent design or even Holocaust denial. Holocaust denial predates postmodernism, and is careful to copy the rationalist, empirical, scientific habits of cool inquiry, even as it degrades them. Intelligent design is a pseudo-scientific belief as well, not a counter to rationalism but a partial concession to it, instigated by a legal and social framework that makes untrammelled belief in a young Earth more difficult. Kakutani's proposed mechanism of universal 'deconstruction' cannot be traced geographically: Holocaust denial is most prevalent in the Middle East, and a belief in intelligent design in the American South. Not locations where Derrida enjoys a wide readership.

The fact that intelligent design flourishes in the same places where 'people with college degrees were gravitating towards cities, while rural areas slipped behind economically' is mentioned only in passing. This precursor agent to Trump really needs more attention. The divide between city and country, localists and globalists, 'somewheres' and 'anywheres' has been theorised as the great cultural clash of our time. It is also a clash where – and I think this is under-appreciated – language is one of the key battlegrounds. When the knowledge economy and its adjuncts take the spoils and the dignity of labour disappears, it makes sense that a revolt against this state of affairs is an unlettered one, the linguistic equivalent of a dirty protest, crass and deliberately offensive, wilfully ignorant, and aimed right at the mores of, say, the chief book critic of *The New York Times*.

TOTAL DEPRAVITY

They shall take up serpents;
and if they drink any deadly thing it shall not hurt them;
they shall lay hands on the sick, and they shall recover.

Mark 16:18

One night John Stephen Toler dreamed that the Lord had placed him high on a rock cliff, overlooking a forest-filled valley. He had this vision while living in Man, West Virginia, where some of the townsfolk thought he was a hell-bound abomination; he countered that God works in different ways. The mountains were where he sought sanctuary, so he felt no fear; but as he watched, all the trees he could see were consumed by wildfire. It was incredible, he said, to see 'how quick it was devoured', and the meaning of the parable was clear: the forest was Man and the fire was drugs, and when the drugs came to Man, that was exactly how it happened – it was devoured 'so fast, that you didn't even see it coming', he said. We were in Huntington, West Virginia, and by now John Stephen Toler was in recovery.

Huntington, the second-largest city in West Virginia, once had a population of more than 100,000 people, but that number has reduced to around 48,000, and almost one-quarter of these, some 12,000 citizens, have either latent or active substance-use disorders. In a local coffee shop (the owners incongrous Australians), the woman behind the counter mentioned this affliction, and said, 'But everywhere has problems, doesn't it?' Not so oblivious as it sounds. An incurious visitor could notice nothing amiss in the city, except its absences. The half-empty streets look rangy and architecturally relaxed. There are plainclothed sex workers, who sit on the steps of churches, and homeless men pushing trolleys, but for the most part the epidemic is so unnoticeable it is almost subterranean.

The back room of an outreach programme called First Steps had become a makeshift confessional, and John Stephen Toler and I were making use of it. First Steps was decorated with the distinctive paraphernalia of recovery: flyers with hopeful clip art, polystyrene cups, wristbands marking time and achievements – but in West Virginia treatment was too common to trouble with euphemisms. The centres were in indiscreet locations. They had open-fronted windows, road-side signs with changeable letters (the same kind churches use), unambiguous names. It was the drugs – they were mainly opioids – that were hidden. There was a whole interstitial city in Huntington, in semi-abandoned buildings, on gas-station patios, under bridges or behind dumpsters.

Huntington's nadir (so far) came on 15 August 2016, when there were twenty-eight overdoses in four hours, two of them fatal. Most were in the surrounds of the Marcum Terrace public housing estate, a cluster of low-rise apartments that distil social problems. A friend, a journalist, was in town not long after this date. She was kept briefly housebound by bad weather, and when the spell of filthy rain broke into a clear, warm day, she went for a walk. She said the streets were nearly empty – Huntington's sylvan parkland, some of it stretching to the banks of the Ohio River, was left to the white-tailed deer. In houses and apartments, a force held sway that was stronger than the elemental drive towards the sun.

John Stephen had overdosed years ago, on some other hot day, not in August. His mother found him in a car with closed windows, not breathing – an event commemorated in a tattoo, 'Life Goes On', shaped like the graph of a pulse sensor. He was twenty-four when we met, but apologised for looking older 'because of the drugs', enough years of use to place a permanent furrow on his brow. His own addiction seemed indistinguishable from the regional misfortune, as if they had gone through parallel entropies – before he became a liar and thief, before he caught his felonies in Atlanta, Georgia, he was known for being so helpful. 'Everyone knew John Stephen Toler,' he said (adding, 'Not because I'm a whore'). He was bisexual and did not hide it. Not uncontroversial in Man, but for some reason, the homophobes made exceptions. 'There's no fear in this queer,' he said. 'No shame in my game. You don't have to like me, but you do have to respect me.'

He had since been to 'hell's basement'. 'We're the fuck-up of fuck-ups,' he said. Addiction was a 'disease of more'. In one 24-hour period, he lost his car, house, job, husband and dog, and then went to jail. Both his parents had substance-use disorders, on and off, his father more on than off. Unless you were a coal miner or in the medical field, it was hard to make it in life, and the coal jobs were not what they were. Man had succumbed so quickly because it was a 'shithole', he said, small enough to miss if you blinked while driving down the four-lane. The money had gone with the coal, and people began selling dope to get money, and then selling dope to get dope, and then selling dope to do dope. Dealing meth became a quick way to make a living, and dealers would use it and get addicted. 'But what about all the initial customers?' I asked. What created the demand in the first place? Why were opioids a bigger problem than meth almost everywhere, and especially here? Why had this happened all over Appalachia?

Beyond hazarded guesses, John Stephen Toler did not know.

Drugs are as societally influential as any other widespread technology. Pharmacology leaves its mark on historical periods as surely as politics does, and the effects and side-effects of millions of doses imprint beyond individuals and into the consciousness of entire eras. Modernity divides into these dynasties: the turn of the twentieth century ruled by morphine, then the amphetamine ascendancy of World War II, a tussle between cannabis and LSD following, the 1980s buoyed by cocaine's confidence… Prozac and MDMA, Valium and Quaaludes – all have a cultural impact far beyond those consuming them.

The influence of opioids on the rural United States eclipses these precedents. Perhaps only London in the throes of the Gin Craze or Imperial China after the Opium Wars could compare. This new phase, described as 'the opioid epidemic' (seldom capitalised), has different characteristics. It has been so frequently outlined by numbers that there is an accompanying complaint: that, like the old irony about deaths and statistics, these factoids muffle rather than amplify the tragedy. But the calamity is on a scale that cannot be quantified by other means.

Graphed by year, overdose deaths form a precipitous climb, and at its peak (2017) are 70,237 dead Americans. Publications present this funerary Everest as part of a mountain range of comparable mortalities. The overdose death apex is taller and steeper than that of guns, dwarfs car accidents and breast cancer, is a head or more over the total US battle casualties of the Vietnam War and shades the AIDS epidemic at its most severe. Opioids by themselves have reduced the average American life expectancy for the first time outside a war.

Beyond the numbing accountancy, the epidemic has done little to impress itself onto the wider American culture. So far, OxyContin has produced no Hogarth, no Coleridge, no De Quincey, no *Easy Rider* or *Drugstore Cowboy*, no *Junkie* or *The Long Weekend*. There is no country-music equivalent of Bowie's Berlin period, or not one with any wattage. There is some book-length journalism, a sliver of fiction, some recovery-themed Christian hip-hop and, perhaps by analogy, the zombie-themed television series *The Walking Dead*. Then a blank. The destruction of much of working-class America by opiates and opioids has happened silently. There seems almost nothing creative to say about it, or no way to say it.

Geography contributes. Heroin has made a modest comeback in New York City, where, along with pain pills, it fills a bit part in polypharmic alt-literature. But opioids have hit hardest in the parts of the United States that are spare and wooded, and the country does not speak to itself in the voice of these places. Visiting the heartland, you catch a drawl in hospitality workers straightaway – wait staff and laconic barkeeps with a narcotic film over their eyes, repping a parodic version of laidback regional charm. One restaurateur couple in Lexington, Kentucky, opened a diner called DV8, focused on addiction recovery. Before that, thirteen of their employees died from addiction in ten years. Drugs were so unavoidable that recovery had to be integrated into the branding to contain the problem.

In Ohio, I met a lawyer, fresh from her garden, whose practice had become largely drug-adjacent. 'This fentanyl and carfentanyl is a national security issue,' she said, wiping her soily hands on her jeans. She was talking about the ultra-powered synthetic opioids, first manufactured for end-of-life care and veterinary anaesthesia, that killed most efficiently. 'It's coming from China, and someone should look at that, because they are killing us.' At first this seemed flatly racist, but the idea of a reverse, twenty-first-century Opium War, the colonised's revenge, was too interesting to stop thinking about.

In chemical terms, carfentanyl is as mortal a threat as nerve gas – more poisonous by median lethal dose (one nanogram) than the venom of the Mojave rattlesnake. It was once unregulated, but after containing its production, the Chinese government made a pointed statement:

1. America consumes 80 per cent of the world's opioids.
2. China, a country in which these substances can be purchased online at wholesale prices, does not have an opioid problem.
3. If America has an opioid problem, it is not because of pharmaceutical imports but American-manufactured prescription drugs.

All true. At the heart of this domestic consumption is the region of Appalachia, set in mountainous seclusion between Kentucky, Virginia, Pennsylvania and West Virginia. Appalachia, when it is thought of at all, occupies a kind of 'herrre be dragyns' place on the mind map of most Americans, occupied by doodled stereotypes: coal, hillbillies, *Deliverance* playing on repeat. Opioid addicts were just added to the stereotypes, a single letter changed to neologise them as 'pillbillies'.

West Virginia is especially overlooked, as though it is the Appalachia of Appalachia. Since the late 2000s, it has used this cover to make something like a state-wide suicide attempt. It was not just that West Virginians overdosed; West Virginia itself overdosed. In the six years between 2007 and 2012, drug wholesalers shipped 780 million hydrocodone and oxycodone pills into its borders. The town of Williamson, Mingo County (population 2900), stocked 10.2 million hydrocodone pills and 10.6 million oxycodone pills in its two small pharmacies. In 2008, in the nearby hamlet of Kermit, the same wholesaler supplied 5624 prescription pain pills for every one of the town's 400 residents.

Some of this pill pyramid was taken away (the editor of the Williamson local newspaper tried to persuade me that Kentucky 'out-of-towners' were to blame), but most doses were consumed locally. Then they were added to. West Virginia was a net importer, and into the pile came the product of Florida pain clinics, spirited via the highways (the Greyhound buses taking this route are nicknamed 'The OxyContin Express'). The merchandise of heroin dealers in Cleveland and Detroit and Indianapolis came over the hills, until the valleys and hollers of Appalachia seemed to fill like bowls.

When problems are as regionally pervasive as this, people start to impugn the landscape. Here that means the mountains surrounding, which incubate clannishness and remove. The ranges did not look sinister to me – they lifted foliage to a height and angle where the leaves pixellated the sunlight – but you could trick yourself into believing that their topography created something cursed in the benighted places of their steppes. People, even Appalachians themselves, sometimes spoke about locals as though they were hill tribes, encamped at a distance from the modern world.

There was a streak of residual Celtic fatalism that was not just mythic. The Democratic West Virginia Senator Joe Manchin was fond of saying that West Virginia had 'more veterans per capita, fought in more wars, shed more blood, lost more lives' than any other state. It was no longer true, but widely believed – he was not the only person I heard say it – and Manchin also claimed that West Virginia had 'done all the heavy lifting. We mined the coal that made the steel that built the guns and ships, built the factories, built the middle class that gave you the quality of life you have today.' Even in this telling, it was a scorned effort nationally.

If there was something corrupting in the mountains, it was the coal. Coal was at the heart of the opioid epidemic. It was extracted from the land, but also made extractions from those labouring for it. Coal has killed West Virginians in subtle and various ways for well over a century. It bowed them, it crushed them; it took their sinews and their lungs. As late as the 1920s, Many Appalachian coal-miners were still boys, as young as eight, preferred because their hands were small enough to work the seams. If these boys were severely injured or killed, the conveyor belts did not stop. After the whistle blew at the end of the shift, the gore and body parts (traumatic amputations were frequent) would then be collected.

In 1921, a series of armed labour disputes known as the West Virginia coal wars culminated in the Battle of Blair Mountain, where miners armed with rifles fought pitched battles with Pinkerton agents, the army and the police. Together these combatants fired more than one million rounds at one another. The coloured neckerchiefs of the resisting miners originated the term 'redneck', and the confrontation means the Second Amendment of the Constitution is locally sacrosanct. In most places, armed defence against government tyranny is a hypothetical. In West Virginia, it is a memory.

Still, the twentieth-century union bosses were accomplices to coal's murders. Black lung was understood early, and too well, and when mechanised drills were introduced, the coal dust they produced was finer, so inhaled more deeply, and killed men with the same efficiency that made the mines more productive. *Appalachian Magazine* records that the legendary United Mine Workers of America leader John L. Lewis 'decided not to raise the black lung issue because it might impede the mechanization that was producing higher productivity and higher wages'. Variations of this inhumane calculation persist.

I had not, before coming to Huntington, ever heard of a 'coal doctor' before, but this profession has a long history, rarely an honourable one. Most coal camps were lonely, rough places with few services, and coal doctors were rugged men who travelled long distances to provide medical aid to the workers. They were often chancers, and have retained some of this quality to this day. Not long ago, miners would finish their work and rise to the top of the pit to find a physician, ready to hand pills to any man with

pains. As the unions faltered and their protections were stripped
away, time spent sick became time unpaid, or an invitation to be
laid off. Pain management was no longer just optimum, it was
indispensable, and then addictive.

Around the same time organised-labour laws were weak-
ened, a company called Purdue Pharma 'invented' OxyContin,
which meant taking a powerful opioid analgesic, giving it a slow-
release coating that could be circumvented easily, concealing its
potential for abuse, and marketing it aggressively to working-
class communities increasingly unable to afford preventative
medical treatment for chronic pain. Its supposed regulators at
the Federal Drug Administration were bribed or lied to, and
it was disseminated through profiteering doctors. The City of
Huntington has sued Purdue Pharma and other companies that
committed these abuses, trying to force them to take responsibility, so far without success.

In the First Steps back room, a man called Steven Little told
me a version of all of this, but before he even spoke, his eyes
hinted at his private history: he was a pastor and he was a former
addict. A quintessentially Appalachian combination, and one
that let him speak with spiritual gravity. He was from Kentucky
but had come to Huntington on a calling.

'Appalachia has always been a familiocentric region,' he said.
'And when you have families dependent on steel and coal, and
those resources and jobs are taken away, you're still left with
the families. And families still have to provide for each other,
and you get the release of a multi-million dollar product –
OxyContins – whereby you can make a quick sale, and make
a big buck, and you can still provide for your family. It was the
perfect storm of events. The coal and the steel was taken away,

and to some extent, the ease to sell dope was introduced around the same time.

'This multi-million-dollar, hundred-million-dollar advertisement campaign was based upon false research: that Oxycontin was the miracle drug, that it's not addictive. And so you get this mass push, and this influx of this highly addictive substance into this community. Where there's already this hole that has to be filled – nature abhors a vacuum, so it will fill itself with whatever it can.'

That hole was present in his own experience: teenaged flashbacks to childhood molestation, hanging with the bad crowd in high school, years of snorting Oxy (though diabetic, he hated needles), recovery, complacency and then a slip. He decided to let loose for a night and within a few hours had a mistress/drug dealer (his 'adulteress,' he called her in recollection, though without judgement), and within a week a $1000 habit. All this while his wife was pregnant with their first child. They separated; he moved the other woman into his former marital home. One morning he came back and the house was stripped; everything was gone, stolen. He fell down on his knees in the garage and asked for higher help.

Pastor Little told me how once he had been waiting at his dentist's office, early for an appointment, and the technician had offered him magazines. He told her he was good for now, but she said that if he wanted some entertainment, he could look out that window there, and probably see some of them nasty old druggies, shooting up behind the dumpster. Here was an opportunity, and seeing as he had some time to kill … She was in tears by the time he had finished his story – he had once been one of those nasty old druggies behind the dumpster. Next visit she buttonholed him. She was volunteering with addicts. Something called Project HOPE.

Superficially heartwarming – but why did a worker in the medical field need a conversion experience to understand basic care? She should have known better; Huntington was full of doctors and nurses who should have known better. They treated substance-use disorders grudgingly – First Steps clients sometimes copped undisguised disdain – and there was a resilient community belief that overdose victims should only be revived a certain number of times (a three-strikes system was mooted), or not at all. Facebook comments on overdose stories were best avoided.

Pastor Little had been doing a survey on first responders and compassion fatigue. 'I think those not in the recovery community assume – wherever that assumption comes from – assume it is a moral sickness, it is a moral impairment. Even the technician lady. She said, "If they really wanted to quit, they would quit."'

He was clinical, unemotional, but not cold. 'I think studies now suggest it's not so much a moral deficiency as it is a combination of biological and cultural deficiencies. Like I told you before, not everybody who comes out of a broken home has addiction, but 80 to 90 per cent, according to Adverse Childhood Experiences scores, come out of broken homes.'

Take the psychological test called the Adverse Childhood Experiences Study ('Did you often or very often feel that … you didn't have enough to eat, had to wear dirty clothes, and had no one to protect you?') and it delivers something called an ACE score, which sounds crude, but predicts addiction and chronic disease with a subtlety and precision that seems almost cruel.

'They're broken down into different categories. I have five,' said Pastor Little. 'Terry may have seven or eight.' Five was very bad. Eight – that was almost off the charts. It was a multi-cause mortality risk. Not many eights were alive past sixty.

Terry ran First Steps.

I liked Terry Collison a lot. One of her friends had cajoled her into this line of work, but she was a natural, and everyone could tell. Every morning she opened a special website that posted mugshots of recent arrests, to see if any of her charges were in the jail. It was getting overcrowded, but most of the criminals weren't too dangerous. People stole strange things here, she said, like patio plants and garden furniture, failures of risk–reward ratio, when Huntington homes were so often protected by cameras and firearms. Only the substance-affected would chance a bullet for a concrete gnome.

The police had not been called to First Steps in many years, and when we talked, Terry would keep one ear open to the other room, where the clients were. If she caught the keening note that comes before an argument, she would keep our conversation going as she got up, and then from beyond the door ... 'I've asked you to stop cussin', and you know what happens if you don't – you leave.' Response unintelligible, tone sheepish. She told me that on one occasion a client had threatened her, and she had only smiled – her smile still has trace quantities of the hippie she used to be – and said, 'Try me, punk.' The real danger, she said, came not from the person threatening her, but from all those men leaping to her defence, escalating something that didn't merit escalation. They loved her, and she loved them. She called them her babies.

In our meeting, the raised voice came not from someone with a substance-use disorder, but a young, floridly psychotic woman, who had been sieved out of the health service and ended up here, where she was not supposed to be. Someone had stolen her cherry red BMW, she kept saying. There was no cherry red BMW.

Not everyone was a candidate for recovery, and sometimes these individuals (who were most commonly men) felt distanced from society, like divers on the end of a line. There were a few rough sleepers out in tents by the Ohio River, and one man, when he had his history tabulated, was found to have been sheltered for only three of the last fifty years. He kept all of his possessions in a cart. The homeless still had phones, and Terry would return from a short trip to find individuals sitting against the outside wall, tethered to the power outlet.

Terry's office window looked out onto 7th Street, and she would commentate the passing parade, telling the stories of the men and women she knew. 'There is a pimp who rides on a motorised cart,' she said, but we did not see him. 'That's one of our little prostitutes' – a woman with a too-tight ponytail, a former student at Marshall, Huntington's university. Good grades, very intelligent, from a good family. Kept a needle in her bra and used it until the point broke off.

Sex workers did not dress the part in Huntington – they were identified by their location, especially those church steps, where they were not shooed away. A local television news service, which Terry maligned for its sensationalism, illustrated its reporting on sex workers with a red stiletto, and she scoffed at the thought. 'I mean, can you imagine,' she said. 'No one in Huntington is wearing red stilettos.' It was as fictive as the BMW.

We went for a drive around Huntington. We saw the women who glanced up at the sound of a car. We saw Marcum Terrace: looking insoluble, overhung by some skeletal trees. A gas station where someone had been shot. The Springhill cemetery, hilly and full of running animals in the late afternoon. We did not gawk at the headstones, seeking overdoses. Instead we went to see the memorial for the Marshall crash, an austere monolith where visitors had laid tributary offerings: fan paraphernalia, Mardi Gras beads, a football so old and dusty it looked made from stone as well.

The Marshall crash was perhaps the most poetic cause I heard proffered as the root of Huntington's opioid crisis. In 1970 the local college suffered what Wikipedia calls 'the worst sports-related air tragedy in U.S. history'. The football team's plane clipped a mountain forest on a hazy November day, and all the players were lost. Coaching staff and a team doctor, too. Houses dyed their sheets black and hung them out the windows. The first-choice Marshall team, the Herd, had to be reconstituted from shocked freshmen. Some had never played before. They lost.

The people who told me this origin theory, predicated on 'heartbreak', seemed to only half-believe it, as though they found out at some point during the telling that they were really discovering the limits of their own memories. The Marshall crash had not created Appalachian melancholia; it was just the first true piece of it that they could recall. Before then, the penury and isolation were entrenched enough for America to mistake them for something pure.

Travel writers visited like it was a foreign land, and in the nineteenth century, expeditions from missionaries and music-ologists tried to divine the traces of some white Shangri-La. I was told of petroglyphs at a place called Indian Caves, written in some ancient relative of Gaelic, left by 'Irish missionaries who arrived centuries before Leif Erikson'. It was a fake, but a fascinating one: the hoaxer imagining the earliest kernels of colonisation among West Virginia's Caucasian 'primitives'.

Not all the atavism was fabricated. There was still a primeval sense of suspicion in Huntington, and there were local behaviours and customs that Terry would recount, smiling and rolling her eyes. She detested Trump, and she thought the prospect of the coal-mining industry returning to Huntington was farcical. There was a kind of magical thinking to this notion. A cohort really believed it, so much so that coal miners often refused to retrain for other occupations. If things were done the old way, then the old ways would return. This Luddism was exasperating. But I came to believe it was correct.

The 'new' jobs would not be the same calibre of the old, unionised mine jobs. Pretending they would be – that was the real pretending. The whole culture of West Virginia is set up to valorise this labour. The service industries were there to serve the mines. Mining was not just prized – it was prized by demeaning other jobs, jobs done by workers with soft hands. There are many families with three generations of coal miners; few will have a fourth. West Virginians have loved the things that kill them for a long time, and it is a love that can be respected as a form of resistance and commitment. Coding cannot provide this fatal romance.

One tentative suggestion, frequently made in Huntington, is that the crisis has had a silver lining for Appalachia. It has led to the thawing of some signature emotional frigidity. It was impossible to maintain stigma on such a scale. Eventually there were too many social lepers to shun (though there were hold-outs who tried). Addiction has finally created a real sense of community, and the beginnings of a proper public-health response. And then following the silver lining was another cloud: the drug war is becoming more therapeutic and less punitive as the victims change from urban blacks to rural whites.

I went to church before leaving. Each week, Pastor Little went to an interdenominational prayer meeting, partly addressed to the opioid crisis, and he invited me along. But he had morning car trouble, and a few other pastors cancelled, and by the time I reached the brick-veneer temple (everything in Huntington seemed to be brick veneer, even the strip clubs) and descended to the crypt – past a stack of evangelical magazines, their covers complaining about 'progressive perniciousness' in the classroom – there was just me and two pastors, Pastor M. and Pastor B., and the meeting was cancelled.

We stayed to talk anyway, sitting at folding tables eating muesli bars and drinking coffee with French vanilla creamer. Pastor M. was a Nazarene, and a former wrestler who let you know this with his handshake. He had grown up in Kentucky, and when he went to school in California, the other pupils asked if he was used to wearing shoes. Pastor B. was from the Church of God. There are about eighty different organisations called the Church of God around the world, and once, he had been invited overseas by a different Church of God, and after arriving realised it was a cult, and they realised they couldn't have him preach, and everyone was stuck trying to be polite.

There was usually a 'no theology' rule at the interdenominational meeting, to prevent arguments, so I joked that we could talk theology if they wanted, seeing as the meeting was cancelled.

We spoke about the concept of total depravity. This is the idea, central to the harder forms of Calvinism, that since the Fall humanity's sin is absolute, and no individual can be redeemed by their actions. Humanity is so iniquitous it is pointless for us even to attempt to avoid sin, and the most extreme forms of this idea suggest we are unable even to accept God's grace. Worship is cowering; God's will and fate are indivisible. Individual will is near-meaningless, and the world can only stew in corruption until its apocalypse.

Set against this are the Wesleyan ideas that underpin Methodism. Heaven is distant (it seems almost an afterthought sometimes to this school), and man's duty is to make the earth as Godly as it can be. This is achieved through a series of steps, and I realised, rather sluggishly, that the step-based treatment programmes I had encountered shared a common source in these ideas, much like Alcoholics Anonymous.

There are denominations within recovery that mimic these theologies as well. Pastor Little told me that some of the pastors (I was not sure if Pastors M. and B. were among them) believed that God could cure addiction by prayer alone, and there were jonesing supplicants at the altar every week. Medically assisted recovery was frowned upon by some who insisted on staying 'clean', and even among the medicated there were differences: some medically assisted recovery groups rejected methadone, while others endorsed its use. Recovery, addiction and religion seemed to swirl together. It was a pious place, where the treat-ment centres were often run out of churches.

Appalachian Christianity was splintered and strange. It had once been considered almost heretical, and Pastor B., who was not from here, had taken some time to understand it. Parishioners were very particular – they complained when he wore jeans – and changes to the service or the sanctuary were treated as near-blasphemies. 'Someone might have put money in to help build that sanctuary fifty years ago,' he said, 'and they feel like they own it.' There were still small churches in the hollers where the congregation would handle venomous snakes or drink poisoned Kool-Aid. There were feuding churches, sometimes even of the same denomination. He had heard a story, years ago, of a visitor to a small town who had sought out a Baptist church on a Sunday, and found two, almost identical, on either side of a road. The alderman greeted him: 'Are you a Democrat or a Republican?' When the man replied that he was a Republican, the alderman pointed across the street and said, 'Over there'.

'There is a saying that in West Virginia, everything is polit-ical but the politics,' Pastor B. concluded.

Pastor M. told me about an early Pentecostal missionary, a barely tolerated presence in some mining outpost full of hard men. They ignored him, and let him know he was ignored, until one day the whole camp arrived en masse to his tent, bending the brims of their hats in their hands, asking to join his 'congregation'.

'May I ask,' said the missionary, 'what made you change your minds?'

'Well,' said their leader, 'we have been poisoning the water in your well, and as you are unaffected, we figure you must have something to teach us.'

AT THE GATEWAY TO CAPE FEAR

B y the time I reached North Carolina, Hurricane Florence had been upstaged. It was, as the president had said, 'tremendously big and tremendously wet': it had generated more rainfall than any weather event in the East Coast's history, dropping 30 trillion litres of water – one town received more than 30 inches of rain in two days. But that was before Hurricane Michael, the strongest storm to hit the United States mainland since 1969, made landfall in Florida. Michael all but monopolised the nation's attention, so the clean-up still going on elsewhere continued anonymously.

Hurricanes in the Atlantic are allocated names before they even exist, which gives them an air of inevitability. The lists of these names are alphabetical. Recycled through seasons, they repeat every six years. 'Florence' had been in use since 1953, and only one other hurricane name had been on rotation as long. There will probably not be another storm called Florence. After this, the name is expected to finally be retired. It has caused a degree of damage that will be associated with distress.

There are regions of the United States more storm-afflicted than the Carolinas, but their easternmost longitude, networks of barrier islands and long rivers do make them unusually vulnerable. Rain swells the blackwater of the Cape Fear River to unfeasible heights. Further north are the Outer Banks, the islands off the coast of North Carolina; and Highway 12, the exposed and fragile-looking road that makes a tenuous link from Cape Hatteras to the mainland. It has been damaged so many times by rising waters that it may soon be abandoned to the seas and replaced by ferries.

North Carolina is also made susceptible by its politics. It was the most progressive state in the South before Republicans gained control over the state's upper and lower houses in 2010. They had waited since 1870 for this double, and began peeling back environmental legislation post-haste. They did not, as the late-night TV host Stephen Colbert joked, make it illegal for scientists to talk about climate change. But scientists were prohibited from forecasting sea-level rise into the future when that could affect real estate prices.

This was cartoonish, but not so different from what other legislatures were up to. Just two days before Michael made landfall, the Intergovernmental Panel on Climate Change released an urgent report warning that 'rapid, far-reaching and unprecedented changes in all aspects of society' would be required to prevent dangerous levels of global warming. It wasn't going to happen. The 'alarm bells' that kept ringing were treated more like car alarms than fire alarms, their clamour ignored. The world had already decided on its policy through inaction: climate-change mitigation. I wanted to see what it looked like.

It was hard to say definitively if Florence had been made meaner or longer by climate change. But, along with sea bass fisheries moving as far north as Maine, cyclogeneses (the process of cyclone incubation) beginning before the hurricane season proper, and a coterie of other 'hundred-year storms' occurring every few years, it was taste of what was coming. An arrival.

Wilmington, the place known as the 'gateway to Cape Fear', was written up as one of the towns worst hit. The roadside woods en route still tasted wet and close; there were piles of smouldering wicker in fresh clearings, and earthmovers still working among the trees. The debris was arranged almost tastefully. The subsiding water had left behind tonnes of silt on the forest floor, which piled up like sandcastles around the trunks. An occasional big softwood had been torn down by the wind: a rough ring count said it had outlasted a century of storms, but not this one. Thousands of fish had been stranded on the tarmac of Highway 40, and had to be hosed away by firemen. There were still many hog carcasses unaccounted for (the storm had drowned 3500 pigs and perhaps three million chickens), and there were rumours they had wound up here in the woods too, or deep in the tea-coloured river. It had reeked for a few days after the weather had fined.

Skewed signage announced the town. The clean-up was at its tail end. There was still a lot to do. Most roads had turned into avenues of chainsawed logs; some displaced root balls were too big to shift yet. Next door to my accommodation, an oak nestled on top of the neighbour's car, as though it was supposed to be there. On the same street a man named Applejack worked the yards with a blower. Applejack had ridden a bicycle all the way from Burgaw, one of the places far away upriver. He was seventy-three but didn't look it, and had eight children, including two sets of twins, the youngest set only five. He had become a double father again at sixty-eight. 'One woman had told me, "Applejack, you stay away from me, the way you make babies!"' he said. His home had been lost, and his family was staying in a shelter, where the men and women were separated, and talking was banned after lights out. When Applejack had entered his storm-ruined house with a woman from Federal Emergency Management Agency, they had encountered a monstrous snake on one of the beds.

Not every house had a tarped roof or boarded windows, but Wilmington's gardens remained covered in swirls of brown leaves. They had turned on the ground – the canopy foliage above them was still green, although it was mid-October, and even in West Virginia, where I had just come from, the seasonal colour was long overdue. The hurricane had jump-started autumn, stripping the leaves that had failed to fall. There were piles of carpet and shattered wood, unbroken windowpanes removed wholesale, upended garden furniture, doors thrown halfway across the block and onto the pavement. At the centre of one pile of detritus I found a soiled and dismantled cat gymboree.

Downtown, the Riverwalk had had its pontoons rumbled. Some businesses right on the threshold of the water had been spared flooding, saved by high shopfronts or control methods. A beachy womenswear boutique was untouched – the river tides had run so high the owners had sandbagged every night for weeks. More than a dozen clean-up workers in hazard masks were busy inside a colonial redbrick with a tower. They pulled black bag after black bag out in a human chain, packing the mess loosely into the tray of a tip truck.

'What is it?' I asked.

'Dust,' said one of the workers, unconvincingly.

It was more likely mould – the building was old, and they were excavating the basement. As I watched, a man sidled up to me, and began talking in a real-life version of hammy expository dialogue.

'That's the old serpentarium,' he said. 'The snake museum. Run by an odd couple. The woman killed her husband. She was acquitted just today, as it happens, by reason of insan-ah-tay.'

Many of the serpentarium's serpents had been collected illegally. As they had improper papers, after the murder they could not be rehoused and had to be euthanised. The serpentarium's owner had been obsessed with weather-related conspiracy theories, and had at one stage dedicated an exhibition wall to the study of chemtrails.

Nearby, one hall full of touristy emporia had survived because it was an old slaughterhouse, with angled floors and a drain underneath. The floors had not seen blood for many years, perhaps a century, but still knew how to sluice away the floodwater.

Wilmington was going to be okay. It had money and a tax base, and was being cleaned up. The worst-hit places were upriver or offshore, at Burgaw or New Bern or Surf City. The 'hold-outs' in these places were often too poor to evacuate, or had nowhere to go. At Fayetteville, the water had swollen to 64 feet. At Rocky Point, freshly built houses were inundated up to the ceiling, and whole pens of locked-in livestock drowned. Piles of coal ash, or 'anaerobic lagoons' – oceans of pig shit that are the by-product of industrial hog farming – all slipped into the waterways.

There was an irony: the places with most media coverage had received the least attention from the storm. I went to

Wrightsville Beach, a wealthy, white-sand coastal community that had become a kind of hurricane media headquarters over the years. There I met Tracy Skrabal, a local coastal scientist. She had a paddleboarder's freckles and a storm-born patience. 'It's kind of bizarre,' she said. 'Here at Wrightsville Beach we've been the eye of Bertha, Fran, Floyd, Matthew – I can't even name them on one hand, the storms since the mid-90s that have raked right across Wilmington. We're sort of set up for the media.'

Jim Cantore was one of the men she had in mind, a Weather Channel star who faced down cyclones in skiing goggles and did a kind of Marcel Marceau act into the gales. 'While he was covering Hurricane Matthew a few years ago,' Skrabal said, 'he went down to Lumberton, a very poor area on the Cape Fear River that was decimated. And he couldn't get out. He had to stay in this really skanky hotel. With no power and no food and no anything. And it probably wasn't that fun.' That was why they came here instead.

This time in Wilmington, the Weather Channel's Mike Seidel had been caught pantomiming, bracing and hunching into the maelstrom – until two passers-by walked calmly behind him. 'It's important to note that the two individuals in the background are walking on concrete,' the network claimed, 'and Mike Seidel is trying to maintain his footing on wet grass, after reporting on-air until 1:00 am ET this morning and is undoubtedly exhausted.' A nice try.

The coverage was so exaggerated it made a kind of appeal to folklore. A weather report was as tall as a fisherman's tale. It was unhelpful in understanding the true threats. 'They spent more time covering the looting of the Dollar General store downtown,' Skrabal said, 'and the prosecution of those looters – who took *diapers* – than they spent getting out into the Cape Fear River.'

There was almost a misplaced romance about it, as if a climate-changed future would be as rugged as a wave-lashed Old Spice commercial. Not all conservatives in North Carolina were true climate-change sceptics – the evidence was becoming irrefutable – though they preferred euphemisms like 'storm adaptation' to the more pertinent 'sea-level rise'. But if the effects of climate change did become more severe, they seemed to be gearing up for a test of mettle, as though the sea was a frontier and we were all pioneers.

Skrabal spent the aftermath of the storm hiding in a closet with two eighty-year-olds, waiting out active tornado warnings. 'Once you do it, there's nothing glamorous about it anymore,' she said. 'My brother used to call me and say, "I wish I was there to ride out a hurricane." Then he went through a smallish one and said, "I've changed my mind." It's life or death. It really is. This last one – I knew I was going to be at elevation. I knew no trees could hit my house. And I still thought, "Why didn't I leave?"'

'These storms are all environmental justice issues,' she continued. 'The scary thing is that those communities on the Cape Fear River – it wouldn't matter if it was a one or a two or a three or a four – they wouldn't have evacuated. They don't have a car. They don't have anywhere to go. They have animals. And they – truly, truly, until you're in it, don't believe you can die.'

The Cape Fear Riverkeeper had lost his house for a second time. It was low-lying, and had been wiped out in Matthew, rebuilt and then wiped out again. 'Does he know better? Hmmm,' said Skrabal. 'I'm not criticising him, but you get the human nature part of this. It was his dad's home.'

That was what made it so dangerous. It was a not a death instinct, the desire to rebuild or to master. It was life, teeming on the banks, but no longer in harmony. The frontier was shifting. 'At some point it is no longer romantic or badass or pioneer spirit,' she said, glancing towards a canal we could not quite see from our vantage point. 'At some point you lose people.'

THE FIRESTARTER-IN-CHIEF

A flag at full mast registers as something of an oddity in the United States. American society is so often in a state of lamentation that an exceptional gesture has become almost the norm, and when you do see a flag lowered, it is sometimes hard to remember exactly what it has been lowered for. The moments of violence or loss blend into one another. Was that the massacre? If so, which one? This does something to time as well: mourning on such a schedule allows little time for reflection, and while the talk is always of 'perpetual outrage', what that really means is fresh outrages. A white supremacist killed eleven people in a synagogue in Pittsburgh, Pennsylvania, on 27 October 2018. Four days later, the event was already downriver in the collective memory.

By now, 'mass shooting in America' is a phrase that carries the same callousing familiarity as 'bombing in Baghdad' or 'historical sex crimes'. Becoming jaded to it is a matter of psychic survival. Contemplation of the real horror would be a full-time occupation, and possibly a lifelong one as well. The motivation for this synagogue shooting was not even notable as a new pathology. There are ample examples of mass shootings as misogynistic or racist terror episodes, from the Charleston church killings (African-Americans) to the Isla Vista massacre (women). Only a few days before the Pittsburgh incident, in Jeffersontown, Kentucky, a man named Gregory Bush tried and failed to open the doors to a predominantly black church, and instead entered a local supermarket and shot dead two African-American shoppers. As he left the crime scene, he 'nonchalantly' walked past a bystander who had drawn a revolver, telling him 'whites don't shoot whites'. Like many white racists, Bush had a black ex-wife, and a son by her.

In Pittsburgh, the controversy rested on presidential responsibility. Had Trump's racialised rhetoric helped inspire the gunman? It had certainly helped inspire the mail-bomber who targeted CNN, Robert De Niro and members of the opposition. The MAGA bomber, as he became known, was a no-hoper desperate for attention, who had tried stripping, body building and petty crime as sources of narcissistic supply. He finally found what he was looking for in Trumpism, and drove around in a van plastered with conspiratoria, set in the busy style of graphic design favoured by schizophrenics. Before his arrest, most 'mainstream' conservative pundits claimed his bomb-sending campaign was also a conspiracy, designed to make Republicans look bad before the elections (as though they needed outside assistance).

Was Trump partly responsible? This question is best answered by its counter: do President Trump's words have no effect on people? At the memorial service, thousands of protesters turned out to make him unwelcome, and tried to communicate love, compassion and tolerance, all the required emotions that Trump can't transmit. Even his supporters in the media worried out loud about the prospect of a eulogistic travesty – after all, a body count is a kind of crowd size – and Ronald Reagan's daughter wrote an article titled 'Let's Stop Asking Trump for Comfort after Tragedies' in *The Washington Post*. Some callers on Fox News Radio agreed, realising belatedly that permanently lowering the national tone might have been a bad idea.

This is the lesson of 'Trump being Trump' that is learned most bitterly: 'inflammatory rhetoric' can set things on fire. It's enraging that this abdication of presidential responsibility is treated as an innovation, as though none of his predecessors had ever had the brainwave that the bully pulpit could be used literally. Most, even George W. Bush, had the verbal facility to demean and abuse from the Oval Office, but recognised the many reasons why this would be wrong, up to and including the kooks and loners and van-men who might find it inspirational (high office knows this division of irregulars by ugly necessity). 'Terrorism is about ideology, but it's also about berks,' the satirist Chris Morris once said, and the dangers of a Berk-in-Chief should be obvious.

But that understanding is not as obvious as it once was, and is not the only matter of principle being unlearned. Alongside the fictional president who can 'fuel the fire' without anyone getting burned, there is an attendant fantasy of a benign ethno-nationalism, which can be implemented without violence. At the same time that Jewish people were being murdered by a neo-Nazi, dictatorship survivors in Brazil were bracing themselves for the imminent election of a neo-dictator. After the fascistic Jair Bolsonaro's election victory, jeeps full of troops rolled through city streets to cheering crowds. At least two Opposition supporters were killed by 'Bolsominions', and a clinic for indigenous people was set on fire. A former colleague of mine, a queer, mixed-race academic who has found herself in effective exile, showed me social-media posts suggesting it was now 'legal' to kill gays and blacks. Something similar had been written by her own brother.

Trump called Bolsonaro to congratulate him, and *The Wall Street Journal* editorialised in the former paratrooper's favour, something that should preclude it from writing about 'freedom' ever again. In São Paulo, the mayor announced that police who shot suspects would receive 'the best possible legal representation'; in Rio, military police stormed universities to remove anti-fascist and pro-democracy material. A former president, Lula, is in jail, and looks set to remain there. He will soon have company.

Could it really be only two years ago that Rio hosted the Summer Olympics? 'We are going to show the world we can be a great country,' Lula said when winning the bid, beating Chicago back in 2009. 'We aren't the United States, but we are getting there, and we will get there.'

The sad part is that he might have been right. In advance of a migrant caravan, Trump ordered troops to be sent to the southern border, and indicated that their numbers could swell to as many as 15,000. 'Operation Faithful Patriot' would begin two days before the November election. 'As a wave of far-right terrorist attacks rock the United States, the Secretary of Homeland Security has been doing PR stunts on the southern border about a group of unarmed Central Americans who are hundreds of miles away in southern Mexico,' the journalist Matt Yglesias wrote on Twitter.

He added that '"The Caravan" is intended as a political distraction from the substance of Trump's economic policy but it also serves as a very real distraction for the actual government, making it harder for people to do actual work.'

But this is the actual government, and this is their actual work.

THROUGH THE HATE TUNNEL

But in silence, in dreams' projections,
While the world of gain and appearance and mirth
    goes on,
So soon what is over forgotten, and waves wash
    the imprints off the sand,
With hinged knees returning I enter the doors,
    (while for you up there,
Whoever you are, follow without noise and be of
    strong heart.)

Bearing the bandages, water and sponge,
Straight and swift to my wounded I go.
                —*Walt Whitman, 'The Wound-Dresser'*

I f you are not with me by the end of this, I understand. Some of you may not make it to the close of the paragraph, and that's fine. We can meet later, when and if you have forgiven me for a belief that is not just a lapse in taste, but a failure of moral judgement as well. Here it is: I think the

most exciting contemporary painter working in America today
is former president George W. Bush.

I do not hold this belief ironically. (Sometimes, I wish I
did.) I do not appreciate the art of George W. Bush (the art of
George W. Bush! Even the phrase sticks in your eye) in the so-
bad-it's-good way you can enjoy the singing of the tone-deaf
former *American Idol* contestant William Hung, or the films
of Ed Wood. I appreciate it in a so-good-it's-good way, just as
Frank Zappa thought The Shaggs' naive music was 'better than
the Beatles'.

At least I have company. The Bush oeuvre has been surprisingly well-received by critics – I share clandestine favourites
with a former lecturer in fine art, and when I confessed my secret
shame with an art PhD, he said only, 'I prefer the early-period
Bush.' True, neither of these fans made a special trip to Tempe,
Arizona, to see the paintings in person, but I went half in the
hope of finding some unreproducible element in the physical
works, something that might repel me, an aura that could inoc-
ulate against the daubings of a war criminal.

Back in 2003, the satirical site *The Onion* ran a piece called
'Bush to Lovely Chilean Ambassador: "I Must Paint You"', and
that was the whole joke, just George W. Bush painting. When
that came true, they ripped the heart out of it anew in 2014:
'George W. Bush Debuts New Paintings Of Dogs, Friends, Ghost
Of Iraqi Child That Follows Him Everywhere'. The best satire is
prescient, and this was again on the mark. This latest exhibition,
Portraits of Courage, features portraits of ninety-eight wounded
combat veterans – and, this part is unsaid – that George W. Bush
sent to war. His subjects were injured during misadventures in
Iraq and Afghanistan. He was responsible.

The question of separating 'the artist from the art' is tedious and unresolvable, predicated on a false dichotomy that positions art as always morally improving. But these unique circumstances re-enliven it. If history has granted artists a licence for transgression, can it do the same for the artist who invaded Iraq? This catastrophic act of illegal belligerence was a war of aggression, what the Nuremberg Judgment called 'not only an international crime; it is the supreme international crime, differing only from other war crimes in that it contains within itself the accumulated evil of the whole'.

This is a different order of moral error from alcoholism or mistreating lovers. Bush himself has dwelled on the question when considering his artistic hero Lucian Freud, a painter he holds in 'awe'. 'The subject matter is a little disturbing, particularly since some of the models were his daughters,' Bush told *American Way*, the inflight magazine of American Airlines. 'But you have to separate the nature of a person from the talent of the person.'

So far, Bush is not applying this logic to himself, and does not see the need. This autumnal career change is not asking posterity for a mulligan, and if Bush can salvage his legacy, it will be via favourable comparison to Trump, not through art. No filigree of guilt is detectable in his statements, and in interviews he has maintained the just-cause defence. But his paintings are still a moral enterprise, and a very complex one. His real antecedent is not Freud, but Winston Churchill, and it was a historian suggesting Churchill's example that led Bush to pick up a paintbrush. Until that moment, the self-described 'art agnostic' had felt that 'something was missing' in his post-presidential life.

Churchill began painting in 1915, when he was already forty, and later published a book about his hobby. 'When I get to heaven,' he wrote in *Painting as a Pastime*, 'I mean to spend a considerable portion of my first million years in painting, and so get to the bottom of the subject.' Churchill's own war crimes should lead to a different afterlife destination, but the book that inspired George W. Bush to set up his own easel is charming. Thinking alone, Churchill wrote, could not relieve the mind of worry: 'The stronger the will, the more futile the task.' (This sounds like a rebuke of another one-time painter, Adolf Hitler, whose best pictures, of tanks on fire, are suspiciously rosy.) In the British tradition, Churchill was at his best when putting the ocean on canvas – you can see he was thinking about Turner while working on *Sunset Over the Sea, Orange and Purple,* and not quite hitting it, which I like. He also had an amateur's enthusiasm for colour – 'I rejoice with the brilliant ones and am genuinely sorry for the poor browns' – a yen that Bush shares.

By all accounts Bush ran a consultative White House, and his studio practice also shows the influence of counsellors. His work has three distinct periods, reflecting his three most important teachers. The first era is his truly naive beginnings, works that were never intended for public display, and revealed only when his sister's email account was hacked (a coincidence: the hacker was named Guccifer, and the hacker at the centre of Russiagate is named Guccifer 2.0). This series is not my favourite, but I can see why that PhD likes them. Bush was annoyed when they leaked, and said he 'found it very interesting the first painting that came out was the one I painted of myself in the bathtub. I did so because I wanted to kind of shock my instructor.'

These authentic rudiments on canvas resonated beyond their novelty. The critic Jerry Saltz said there was finally something about Bush that he liked. Can a former president really be an 'outsider', in the outsider art sense? But George W. Bush is outside the art world, and perhaps any former leader finds themselves outside the world they knew.

His second period, portraits of world leaders, shows a talent stumbling like a foal. Most impactful was a Munchian, ghoulish portrait of Vladimir Putin – when artist met subject, Putin obsessed over comparing the relative size and power of their dogs, a bizarre but telling detail Bush tried to convey in paint.

The most recent series was completed under the tutelage of the Fort Worth painter Sedrick Huckaby, who has documented African-American life and the Occupy movement in heavy impasto. (The apparent political tension between master and pupil has been negotiated but not explained – Bush does not rate a mention on Huckaby's Wikipedia page, for example.) When Huckaby saw Bush's world leaders series, he suggested pushing on towards 'people that you know that others don't', and suggested that the former president should 'try pushing the limits of colour'. *Portraits* is the result.

The exhibition had toured four cities – had it been popular in Arizona? 'It's not doing as well as we'd hoped, to be honest,' one of the counter staff at the Arizona Heritage Center admitted. The local news station, K-Star, had advertised it, rather awkwardly, to 'valley art and military supporters', but I had the first room to myself. (A detail on entering: I have not before seen a fine art show listing 'Major League Baseball' as one of the sponsors.)

Portraits of Courage opens with Bush narrating a rigid video, to-camera. His speech, even in this context, retains its negative

Pavlovian powers, and the clip was brief enough to play over
and over in the hours I was there. By the end, only one phrase
still registered as words: the former president saying 'the symptoms of post-traumatic stress'. But I was not deterred. In real
life, George W. Bush's paintings are arresting, sometimes moving, and convey an irreducible meaning I still cannot figure out.

He is prolific – this collection of sixty-eight paintings and a
four-panel mural was produced in only a year – but they look
energetic rather than rushed. The painter knows his art history without leaning on the derivative. His eye is, ironically,
more humane than Lucian Freud's, and has its own curiosity,
expressed through an unorthodox palette and means of creating
light (we should be careful about calling this a talent for rendi-
tion). Bush Junior favours 'closely cropped portraits that I hope
give viewers a sense of the remarkable character of these men
and women'. Some subjects sit almost pressed into the frame,
and the colour liberated by Sedrick Huckaby flows out. A golf-
course sky is electric orange, a shoe melds into the dirt in the
same unearthly hue; the strokes are thick and erratic enough to
show naked canvas, and make unconscious symmetries.

He is not great at faces – their off-kilter elongations are the
only true Freudian echo, though a discordant one – but he is
good at facial expressions, a confusing combination. Impasto
holds original positions: a beard is spackled on like cake frost-
ing; pupils are two dabs of mud; one man's under-eyes, hollowed
by torment, are expressed as convex, like a photo negative. Some
of the better pieces centre visages hidden by caps or glasses.
A portrait of Sergeant Daniel Casara falls into this category.
Often, Bush makes light fall on his subject's foreheads as strips
of lacquery cream or rose, but on Casara, it is purple, green,

egg-shell blue, burnt orange, umbery brown, purple and black, an off-colour spectrum coming through the prism of this man's experience. The right side of his face is in shadow, the ear almost silhouetted against the crimson background.

Unseen are Casara's legs, crushed when his armoured personnel carrier hit a mine. The sergeant had twenty-four surgeries, but met Bush through mountain biking. A cynic might think all the close-cropping dodges the question of these broken bodies, but we do see amputations, and sometimes deep fissures from head injuries. Prostheses, though, are usually pictured on the golf course, at the Bush Institute Warrior Open Tournament. In *Sergeant Saul Martinez,* a double amputee flexes his artificial legs as he hoofs a wood shot. The subject has looked up (I bet he sliced it), and the spectators, so scraped out they are almost spectral, follow the ball in flight as well. Martinez's arms and shoulders, in optimistic posture, are bordered in thick white, like 'action' lines on a cartoon.

Overall, the wounded are painted with sympathy, but in the process of overcoming. Bush emphasises the psychological wounds – in part, he says, to diminish stigma – but the faces are harrowed rather than haunted. So *Master Sergeant Scott Neil* depicts a PTSD sufferer in homely nobility. In the book accompanying the exhibition, Neil describes himself as 'through the hate tunnel and on the other side and enjoying being a great American'. True despair is absent; so is disfigurement. After World War I, when George Grosz and Otto Dix drew casualties to try to stop more of them being made, they forced heroless imagery upon the viewer: their subjects had suppurating skin, smashed faces. If, for the Neue Sachlichkeit artists, the 'war cripple' was a metaphor for the Weimar Republic (a 'political mutant',

Robert Hughes called it), Bush's paintings place the United States
as limping, but only between strides.

Had this mild propaganda been controlled, *Portraits of
Courage* would succeed only as a hyper-patriotic salute, a salon
of what the theorists Nicole Markotić and Robert McRuer mem-
orably called 'crip nationalism', where the disabled subject is
invisible, until it benefits the state. But it was not controlled.
Artworks escape their creators, and just as Rage Against the
Machine's anti-imperialist rock music was turned up and used to
torture in Guantanamo Bay, so the former commander-in-chief's
art distorts, and uncovers the lie behind 'mission accomplished'.
Perhaps Sedrick Huckaby's influence has wormed down all the
way into the subconscious.

In the final room was a large mural, depicting members
of each of the United States Armed Forces. Instead of trium-
phal, it was uncannily reminiscent, in feel as well as form, of Joe
Coleman's portrait of the Manson Family.

The militaristic German writer Ernst Jünger had a sensibil-
ity once described as *l'art pour l'art,* but for war. In his novel *The
Glass Bees,* Jünger dwelled on the post-battle defacement and
deformity caused by industrial weaponry:

> The brutal exhibition of severed flesh shocked me … Wasn't
> it an integral part of technical perfection and the intoxi-
> cation of it …? Mankind has waged wars since the world
> began, but I can't remember one single example in the *Iliad*
> where the loss of an arm or a leg is reported. Mythology
> reserved mutilation for monsters, for human beasts of the
> race of Tantalus or Procrustes … It is an optical illusion to
> attribute these mutilations to accidents. Actually, accidents

are the result of mutilations that took place long ago in the embryo of our world; and the increase in amputations is one of the symptoms bearing witness to the triumph of the morality of the scalpel. The loss occurred long before it was visibly taken into account.

Sitting in front of the mural was the only other visitor, a young man, who looked at it intently, while talking on the phone in Arabic. Who was he? What did he think of the work? I never found out – the call continued until I left. I did not have the nerve to interrupt, and did not know what I thought myself. All good art is complicating, and the good art of a world leader more complicating still. Its purpose is to speculate on the unknowable: the nature of power, who we are, why we keep doing this to ourselves. Where logic fails to convey contradictory answers, we turn to aesthetics. Here, a high vantage point and some talent was no closer to producing understanding. Not for the first time, George W. Bush transmitted cluelessness. Only this time it was a melancholy kind, a human cluelessness, which did not transcend culpability, but accidentally confessed to it.

LOSING THE PLOT

The 'Oumuamua is, or was, an interstellar body of unknown origin that permeated our solar system in 2017. It was detected by chance on the Pan-STARRS1 telescope in Hawaii, but it was not until November 2018, immediately before the US midterm elections, that two Harvard scientists released a paper describing the cigar-shaped object's unique properties. One explanation for the 'Oumuamua's unusual flight, they suggested, was that it may be an alien probe or craft originating in a two-starred system of impossible distance.

It has been said that America now produces more news than it can consume, so this potential milestone in humanity's lonely journey through the universe was only half-heralded. Some gee-whiz headlines disappeared into an undifferentiated slurry of events, ever moving, like a spill. If there was any reaction to the UFO at all, it was more like embarrassment than wonder. Godlike visitors in the neighbourhood weren't seeing us at our best.

My own trans-civilisational probe was only into the American elections, but it too took on an unorthodox trajectory. The midterms are enormous, too big for one person to take in.

They encompass all of the House of Representatives a third of the Senate, and governorships and positions in state legislatures as well – they are really thousands of elections, with tens of thousands of candidates, if you count the micro-contests for county commissioners or sheriffs, and take place over hefty stretches of time and distance. While the Senate seats and congressional districts competed over are clearly demarcated, the regions they form together are ill-defined, as though ordained by someone waving vaguely at a map. It all adds up to a fuzzy logic.

I spent the campaign in the Sun Belt, a place that tells a story about the American present (imperfect) and the American future (conditional). The expanse between Florida and California below the 36th parallel north – give or take Virginia – was once poor, whitish and rural, and is en route to being wealthy, diverse and urban. The causes of this change are sometimes obscure and prosaic (one of the key drivers, boringly enough, was the invention of air-conditioning), but the Sun Belt has the added value of not being the Midwest. Like any reporter who also covered the 2016 US election, this trip was partly penance for Getting It Wrong, but I wasn't going to make another pilgrimage to Pennsylvania or Ohio, some of the most journalistically over-explored terrain on earth in recent times. The Midwest's formerly industrial Rust Belt has become the American media's sociological G-spot. (Another mundane explanation: these places are driving distance from New York City.)

'The polls were wrong' has become Donald Trump's retrospective motto, post-2016. Like most phrases in the word cloud that fugs this presidency, it is an untruth. The polls were more accurate in 2016 than they were in 2012, and predicted the popular vote precisely. What was wrong was the interpretation of those numbers: punditry tended to interpret a 1 per cent chance or a 20 per cent chance as a zero per cent chance of winning. Handicapping a victor who had made a taped confession of sexual assault turned out to be hard. Nevertheless, all this was taken as final proof that the media are effete libtards who decant their experience through layers of bias and abstraction, rather than feeling things in their gut, the way a man does.

Among the many sorrows flown from this Pandora's box was a lot of second-guessing. Civil society, or what was left of it, decided to seek the wisdom of fools instead of sages, and ship college graduates out to understand Trump supporters in, well, Pennsylvania. This approach felt inauthentic from the beginning, and exhausted its usefulness quickly. This time I avoided Trump rallies. I don't mind trash talk, or people who hate the media (they're often right), but I wasn't going to stand in a cattle pen acting as a prop, or be cast as the heel in a one-sided professional match, without so much as a folding chair to swing. I revolted against the instinct that a 'Tree. Rope. Journalist' slogan on a dead-eyed good old boy's T-shirt was a garbled cry for help. What started as anthropology ended up as cryptozoology, a fruitless search for the one mythical mountain man who could explain it all.

If this kind of pandering – a dance with strangers – is so important, is the negative version allowed? Can I give my eyewitness testimony? I've spent many months talking to hundreds of Trump supporters, all over the United States, and by tour's end thought them more ignorant, prejudiced and malicious than I did at the beginning. I'm not talking about Republican voters, who often offer caveats and ballot-box habit as mitigation. But *Trump* supporters . . . after a while, I was frankly reluctant to talk

to them. 'The deep state, OK,' I would say, my notebook opening
up like an abyss. Is that admissible, in this festival of anecdata?

Experience in the 'real world' doesn't dislodge the impression that Trumpism is driven by racism. It cements it. Trumpism
does what it says on the tin, and part of the unpleasantness
comes from repetition and recognition. If you've been to the
Balkans or the Middle East, you will be familiar with the style of
trap-doored conversation that takes place when rumour is the
informational gold standard. You are speaking with a seemingly
ordinary, often affable stranger, investing rapport, and suddenly
the talk jacknifes and spills irretrievably into a ravine of batshit
conspiracy. It happens so seamlessly, sometimes in the course
of a single sentence, or a derailing train of thought, that there is
no real way to prepare for it. The topic transitions from sport or
all the rain we've been having to the protocols of the globalists,
without even an alteration in tone. If this happens often enough,
it is demeaning, and if it happens nationwide, you start to fret
about the future of the country involved.

This is not quite the default experience in the rural United
States, but it's close. There was a time – it concluded not long
ago – when I would pay assiduous attention during these dia-
tribes, believing they held hidden gems of importance. Revising
that view was painful, and over the course of the campaign I
found my professional curiosity diminishing, a sensation I had
never experienced before. It was not the violations of truth –
those were bearable. It was the indications that the people
speaking to me (or, more often, at me) didn't really believe what
they were saying at all. If they were over the age of seventy, poly-
medicated and watched Fox News, they were basically mentally
unstable, and would present a tissue of secret high crimes so

incongruent it offered an unusually literal representation of the phrase 'losing the plot'. It was performative, and reminded me of John Steinbeck going to see the 'Cheerleaders', the pro-segregation protesters who abused pupils of colour on their way to school in New Orleans in the 1960s:

> Here was no spontaneous cry of anger, of insane rage. Perhaps that is what made me sick with weary nausea. Here was no principle good or bad, no direction. These blowzy women with their little hats and their clippings hungered for attention. They wanted to be admired. They simpered in happy, almost innocent triumph when they were applauded. Theirs was the demented cruelty of ego-centric children, and somehow this made their insensate beastliness much more heartbreaking. These were not mothers, not even women. They were crazy actors playing to a crazy audience.

I thought of that passage many times, when I switched a car radio to the AM band, or walked into a bar playing Fox News, or asked the right question, or eavesdropped on the diner booth behind mine and caught the high, faltering voice of hatred. I thought of it in Georgia, and Texas, and Arizona, and Nevada. But most of all, I thought of it in Florida.

Before about 1820, the midterms were the most important elections in America. They had a higher turnout than the presidential ballot, and this was partly because structural oddities meant the stakes were higher. That surging feeling came back in 2018. Instead of merely a contest for the House of Representatives and the Senate, it was a referendum on whether the changes wrought by an outlier presidency would be ratified. No one could pretend Donald Trump was an unknown quantity anymore. John Cassidy in *The New Yorker* summed it up this way:

> While the United States remains an economic leader, it appears right now to be spiralling into a miasma of acrimony, post-truth thinking, and violence. The combination of ubiquitous connectivity, unregulated social media, lax gun laws, and rampant political demagoguery is presenting a challenge that our system of government hasn't faced before.

In Florida, a place that looked like the new America in miniature, this description felt most acute.

Florida is a graveyard for liberal political dreams. It is where a contested count gave George W. Bush the 2000 election, and its electoral college votes were decisive for Trump. Its rural counties are retrograde, it is full of addled retirees, and its large Hispanic population raises hopes just high enough to dash them.

The Harvard lecturer Pippa Norris, an expert on the practical business of elections, wrote that domestic and international experts rate the US elections as the worst among all Western democracies. Florida, with its corruption, and incompetence, and voter suppression, and inept Democratic Party 'machine', is perhaps the worst-functioning of all American democracies. 'Mired in recounts' should be printed on the state's number-plates. (It is again mired in recounts as I write.) If the Democrats were going to squander a seven-point polling lead, it would be here.

Statewide, Democratic fortunes rested on four key races, at three different levels of government. There were two House races in South Florida: the 26th and 27th congressional districts. In the Senate, the incumbent was a Democrat, Bill Nelson, and his challenger was the current governor of Florida, Rick Scott, who was trying to go federal. For the vacated governorship, the favourite was Andrew Gillum, the African-American mayor of the state capital, Tallahassee. Gillum was garnering inevitable Obama comparisons, while on Fox News his Republican opponent, Ron DeSantis, had commenced his campaign by asking Florida voters not to 'monkey this up'. That was all you needed to know about DeSantis. All of these Democrats were ahead in the polls. There was a lot to lose, and for a moment they looked intent on losing it all.

These campaigns should have had a single purpose – elect Democrats – but they were fresh from acrimonious primaries, organised by different wings of the party and hostage to the quirks of volunteers. On arriving in Miami, I made a routine enquiry: where could I see the candidates speak? The answer became a four-day odyssey. Early voting had begun, but the Democratic campaign offices I toured looked half-empty and only half-busy. I was given a phone number, which routed to the City of Miami Gardens switchboard. Staff would reference the Miami-Dade Democrats, and then roll their eyes. No one seemed to be in charge. At a critical voting precinct, those handing out how-to-vote cards took me to their leader. He turned out to be a young backpacker who knew no more than anyone else, which was nothing, and had been in Florida only a few weeks.

Where was he before that? 'Spain.'

'I have to say, I haven't had these problems with the Republicans,' I told one campaign manager. 'Well, they're a lot more organised than us,' was the on-the-record reply.

Events had played their part to stymie the organising. Security had increased after mail bombs were sent to CNN and other declared enemies of the president. A Democratic event featuring House Minority Leader Nancy Pelosi had been harassed by an alt-right street gang. (The organiser of the protest turned out to be the head of the Miami-Dade Republicans, Nelson Diaz.) But it was not just lockdown that made it hard to find out what was going on. I tried to speak with a key press officer and had to go through twenty-two different people, almost none of whom had heard of him. Nelson and Gillum were both frontrunners on the morning of election day, and both losers by the end of it. Unusually low turnout in Miami-Dade County was blamed.

I did finally see Gillum speak, in a gubernatorial debate with Ron DeSantis. Sitting outside the venue at Broward College was a middle-aged man in a lawn chair, with a homemade sign reading 'Gays for Trump'. At best he was *a* gay for Trump, and was later misidentified by bumbling online sleuths as the Florida man who had sent those mail bombs. The real suspect was Cesar Altieri Sayoc Jr, a type specimen of 'Florida Man', the distinct species whose natural habitat is outlandish headlines. (Election day offered 'Florida Man Wearing Crocs Gets Bitten After Jumping into Crocodile Exhibit at Alligator Farm'.)

Gillum was the candidate for Floridians, Ron DeSantis the man for Florida Man. 'Racially charged' was the electoral euphemism du jour, and this was one of the most racially charged contests in the land. *The New York Times* wrote about 'racial flare-ups' in Florida, as though the state had a heat rash instead of a racism problem. DeSantis had spoken at events where white supremacists were present. White supremacists made robocalls full of racial slurs targeting Gillum. You could tell it was a grudge match. 'I'm not calling Mr DeSantis a racist,' Gillum said, 'I'm simply saying the racists believe he's a racist,' and DeSantis started as if struck.

Apart from the monkey comment, they clashed over the 'caravan', the group of Guatemalans, Salvadorans and Hondurans making their way through Central America. These individuals were hoping to seek asylum in the United States, and President Trump had ordered thousands of troops to the border to stop them. DeSantis thought the caravan could be an orchestrated invasion designed to smuggle Chinese-made fentanyl over the border. This theory, by conservative standards, was a model of probity.

Most times after a debate, campaign surrogates come out and talk with the media. Here, instead, the Republican Florida congressman Matt Gaetz (himself something of a Florida Man and perhaps the most obnoxious politician in America) started shouting at a Democratic surrogate, creating a kind of undercard fight to the debate's main event. It was so rude, and he was braying so loudly and close to their faces, that reporters, not knowing what else to do, started to laugh.

In October, Gaetz had posted a video 'proving' that the people in the caravan had been paid by the billionaire George Soros. 'Footage in Honduras giving cash 2 women & children 2 join the caravan & storm the US border @ election time. Soros? US-backed NGOs? Time to investigate the source!' he wrote, in the choppy syntax of direct-mail scams. Of course, the video was retweeted by the president. The footage was really from Guatemala, and appeared to show local retailers giving the caravan money in support.

Elsewhere, in Miami, these 'racially charged' conspiracy theories were causing headaches for moderate Republican candidates. In Florida's 26th and 27th congressional districts, they were trying to hang on to Spanish-speaking seats.

The little man on the door had a gold chain and a bald head, round and shiny as a melon, and despite his age and appearance was trying to transmit menace. 'It's RSVP-only tonight,' he said, and couldn't hide his disappointment when I was on the list. Upstairs, in the kind of restaurant where frozen margaritas swirl in an ice machine, the Federated Republican Women of North Dade were hosting an evening with Maria Elvira Salazar, the Republican candidate for Florida 27.

Florida 27 was unusual. Its congressperson, the moderate Republican Ileana Ros-Lehtinen, had resigned, leaving it open. Trump had lost it by twenty points in 2016. Ros-Lehtinen didn't like her chances, and she didn't like Trump. (She once described the president as having a 'warped mind'.) But Salazar, a former Spanish-language TV journalist, was gaining against her opponent, a Democrat called Donna Shalala. It was Shalala, alongside Pelosi, who had been yelled at by the alt-right.

At the front of the room was a banner-sized logo; it was supposed to be a crimson map of Florida emblazoned over a high heel, but instead looked like a communist flag crammed into a shoe. That was ominous. The audience – chaining Virginia Slims, piling buffet plates with free seafood until their hands trembled, one sitting in a walker like it was a throne – was replete with Cuban Americans. These were exiles from Castro, or the children of those exiles. I have heard them nicknamed *momia* by other Spanish speakers, 'mummies' – so right-wing they seem to have emerged from an ancient tomb.

I sat next to a Cuban American named Eva Exposito; she had stopped voting for the Democrats because 'Obama was lazy'. I was trying to unlisten to a confused exegesis on sharia law when a woman in sincere business attire approached, handing me a sheet of paper and a pen. 'We're just checking everyone is registered,' she said, tapping her 'list'.

'This paper is blank,' I said.

'Well, I recognise everyone else,' she said.

Next she 'checked' a young black woman on the other side of the room, before returning to me. This seemed a cheap intimidatory gesture, but it turned out she had just forgotten our first encounter, though it was only five minutes earlier.

Florida 27 is more than 70 per cent Hispanic, but President Trump's 'Mexicans are rapists' outreach program had not salted the earth. In fact, half these people probably agreed with him, and that made Maria Elvira Salazar's job difficult. She was running as a broad-appeal candidate – pro-business, distinct from Trump, willing to call him to account, wanting to do something about climate change. Tonight, she was addressing an audience who did not want her to do any of those things.

She reached the small stage to applause that felt somehow investigatory. Her manner was charismatic, but she was uncertain without an autocue, and her ad-libs clanged. It was a tough crowd. 'I believe we have an opportunity to keep the seat,' she said.

'Miss Shalala is not part of this community. She did not go to school with the Cubans, Haitians, Venezuelans, Colombians … and more Colombians. And of course the Americans.' [Pause for laughter … no laughter.] 'See, I'm trying to be funny,' she continued. The dynamic had gone open-mic night. She looked into the bleak faces of the audience for signs of human warmth and did not find it.

She tried to talk about bipartisanship, and accountability, and the environment (Florida's Republicans have been forced to acknowledge sea-level rise), and in response the room tumble-weeded. Marshland was seized on, but not in the way she was hoping. 'The swamp!' someone called out, and Salazar said, 'Let's not call it the swamp. Let's call it Washington connections.' At one stage she said, 'The difference between Obama and Trump is that Obama knew how to talk. He had finesse,' a sentiment so comically unpopular it seemed almost heroic.

It held together, fractious but lively, until the question-and-answer session. Even then, sanity remained until we hit the caravan. 'These are human beings,' Salazar said, but the audience weren't so sure they agreed.

'It's an invasion!' someone yelled. Here we go.

It was 'not a complete accident that it started two weeks ago', said someone else.

'Soros!' an old Jewish woman cried out, and after one extra-long ramble Salazar let her hands drop. She was curious and exasperated, back to the posture of a journalist instead of a candidate, asking questions instead of answering them. Why would someone fund the caravan? How was this supposed to work?

'If just one person pushes someone … you're in trouble' was the theory. If a border patrol agent beat someone, America would be morally blackmailed into taking 'them'. An orgy of nodding. There was concurrence. There was liberation, something breaking free.

'To create division.'

'Maybe it was CNN that started it.'

'Listen to her – she is a psychologist!'

Salazar made some enthusiasm-free statement about putting people on planes and sending them back home, and finally hit serious applause.

Then people started complaining about their pensions. Obama didn't increase them enough. A room full of migrants complaining the US government doesn't give them enough welfare, all hopped up on Fox News and Facebook videos. Unreal.

I turned to my seatmate in the aftermath. 'Eva,' I said, 'I'm curious – what separates you from those Guatemalans? You were a migrant once.'

'We don't want them,' she said.

'Well, many Americans didn't want you either,' I said.

'We came here legally,' she said.

'Only because of an open border policy. The Mariel boatlift – that was 100,000 people, not 2000 people.'

'We don't want them.'

'And that group was full of criminals, and patients from mental hospitals. "Castro flushing the toilet", people called it.'

'Richard, I'll tell you a little secret. Cubans have always been the Americans' favourites.'

By the wall were two state legislature Republican candidates, Chamber of Commerce types who looked almost as stunned as me. 'What was all that about?' I asked one of them. His business card identified him as 'Jonathan "J.P." Parker'.

'A lot of Cubans got here under a policy called "wet foot, dry foot", where if they made it to the United States they were citizens,' he said. 'And that makes them feel special.'

'I understand that shut-the-door psychology,' I said. 'But these people are slamming the door. A room full of Cubans and Jews, peeling the paint about refugees. I've never seen anything like it.'

He did his best Brooks Brothers smile and touched me on the shoulder before he said, 'Welcome to Miami.'

The Washington Post reporter Dave Weigel is probably the best race-by-race electoral analyst around. All the way back in February 2017, he tweeted, 'Honestly the funniest 2018 result would be: Dems win the majority based on suburbs after reporters spend two years canvassing rural diners.' And that's what happened. Salazar lost, and so did Carlos Curbelo, her partymate over in Florida 26. Curbelo, one of the only Republican congressmen to legislate against climate change, moderated so hard that he seemed reluctant to even encourage people to vote for him. At a town hall I attended, Curbelo was asked what he would say to someone planning to vote for his opponent. He answered, 'Good for you.' Maybe he was throwing it.

Republicans nationwide were bleeding urban and suburban votes. On the ground this was not just noticeable but jarring. Almost any city, no matter how rural or small, starts to produce liberalism. In Louisville, Kentucky, I went into a pit barbeque restaurant and found it selling kombucha on ice. Huntington, West Virginia, has a gay bar (in fact, it used to have two). Anywhere there is a college, or service industries, or nascent diversity, Democrats have a foothold.

Hitting true Trump country, not just isolated pockets, required real mileage, way beyond an Uber from an airport. In Texas, I drove to Tarrant County, which encompasses the city of Fort Worth. This was supposed to be the largest remaining urban 'red' county in the country, and so I kept going, eventually pulling up at a polling station surrounded by parched semi-industrial estates. It had a parking lot full of pick-ups, and looked very Republican, but there was election literature in Vietnamese, and almost everyone casting an early ballot turned out to be a) Hispanic and b) enthused about the Democratic senatorial candidate, Beto O'Rourke. The results showed that Tarrant County is now no longer majority Republican. Of eighty-one urban or semi-urban districts nationwide, eighty are now represented in Congress by Democrats. Beto lost, but ran the closest race against an incumbent Texas senator in forty years.

Phoenix, Arizona, still has some very conservative suburbs, but the voters in Maricopa County sounded most concerned about the tenor of the campaign. The Senate contest was between a bisexual Democrat, Kyrsten Sinema, and a Republican congresswoman, Martha McSally. (The anti-Trump Republican Jeff Flake had announced his retirement, vacating the seat.) The campaign spots on Arizona radio sounded extra venal and stupid.

'I'm shocked at how negative these ads are,' said Raymond Ginther, a Democratic voter, in downtown Phoenix. 'It's as though these people have no redeeming qualities. They're just throwing garbage at their opponents.'

He was unpersuaded by the caravan. 'It's all nonsense. Sending 15,000 troops, at a horrible cost, to prevent 2000 people getting in? It's political horn-blowing.'

Initially, the race was called for McSally, but a late surge from Maricopa County put Sinema over the top. She was part of a record-breaking year for female candidates. In Congress, at least 115 women won. Among the new 'freshmen' class were the youngest-ever woman (Alexandria Ocasio-Cortez), the first Muslim women (Rashida Tlaib and Ilhan Omar), the first Native American women (Sharice Davids and Deb Haaland). Of the Republicans elected to Congress for the first time, only one, Carol Miller of West Virginia, was a woman. Almost all the remaining Republicans were white men.

Today's Republican Party voters are heavily white and rural; by contrast, Democrats are a coalition of the diverse urban and suburban voters, and, increasingly, the wealthy. Measured by median income, the richest House districts in eleven states flipped from Republican to Democratic. According to the election analyst Evan Siegfried, 56 per cent more people under thirty voted than in the 2014 midterms (overwhelmingly for Democrats), and Republicans lost fourteen points of their support among the over-65s. The most significant shift was in female voters. In 2014 they favoured Democratic candidates by four points, but this year that advantage was +19.

The GOP had female trouble, and they knew it. Even in the shadow of Death Valley, Nevada, where Democrats fear to tread, Republicans were trying to soften the appeal of their star candidate. There were billboards all along the unfruitful highway reading 'Women for Hof'. Like Trump, Dennis Hof was a reality-TV show star who had been accused of sexual abuse.

Unlike Trump, he was dead.

He had been found unresponsive by the porn legend Ron Jeremy, the day after two of them had celebrated Hof's seventy-second birthday. Also present at his campaign rally/celebration the previous night were the Republican anti-tax activist Grover Norquist, the disgraced celebrity sheriff Joe Arpaio and Hollywood madam Heidi Fleiss. Public Enemy rapper Flavor Flav had not been present, but was said to be inconsolable.

Hof was now buried – in a cherry red coffin, with a floral tribute that depicted two rabbits making love – but it was too late to remove him from the ballot. County officials would vote on a replacement if he won – and he was still the favourite, meaning the town of Pahrump would rather vote for a dead pimp than a live Democrat. Even a woman who claimed she had been raped by Hof said she would still vote for him posthumously, one of the most extreme cases of 'voting against their interests' ever recorded.

At a strip mall (bail bondsman, chain-link fence, 'For Lease'), I was taking photos of obscured campaign signage when I ran into one of Hof's biggest supporters. He was a Christian consti-tutionalist candidate for lower office called Lance Schaus, and he and his wife were putting up corflutes for his run at Nye County treasurer. His wife was wearing a freshly bedazzled pullover, each rhinestone sitting in a tiny freckle of hard glue, and soon Schaus was in interview mode. He put on a top hat; it was a signature, and did not impede his ability to talk serious policy. He used Hof's and Trump's names interchangeably, so often it went from a slip to a tic. Hof and the president were ratcheting him towards a reluctant social liberalism. There was a place selling cannabis up the road. The brothels were legal, he said, and pastors at the Christian Men's Breakfast he attended most Wednesdays should be focusing on sodomites and adulterers instead. He conceded that the brothels might contain both adultery and sodomy.

Over at Terrible's Roadhouse Casino it was already dark inside, though it was not yet dusk, and at the bar was a woman in late middle age, wearing a Notre Dame college football shirt. She was drinking on the house and playing video poker, not the hallmarks of life's winners, but she was a surprise, a snowbird who had escaped the cold in Indiana. She had raised the sister sitting next to her, and every night before sleep she read the science journal *Nature* and wondered. Her face twisted at the mention of Trump. 'Don't get me started on that man,' she said. 'Have you heard about Hof? Ughh. We vote Democrat, but there are some mighty intolerant people around here. We've been asked,' she continued, looking around, '*to tone it down* when we talk about politics.' Like many women I'd encountered on the campaign trail, she impressed a message on me for broadcast: 'Please, tell the world there is still decency left in America.'

Please tell them we're not all like this. Sometimes these women were first-time voters or former Republicans, but they had been dealing with Trump-like men all their lives.

When election day came, I was in California, where voters were queuing outside libraries and community centres to send a variation on this message. The American electoral system is a chaos of midweek elections, faulty ballots and proprietary voting machines made by companies that no longer exist, so the wait sometimes lasted hours. As with the US healthcare system, the voting system is best understood not as 'broken' but as a sophisticated network functioning for an ulterior purpose, in this case the deliberate disenfranchisement of people of colour. Elsewhere the lines slowed enough that voters had to go back to work, but here the people waiting seemed to draw a sense of solidarity from the wait, as though standing together was the beginning of their collective mission.

'This is the longest I've ever waited for any election, including presidential,' said a woman named Elissa Jhunjhnuwala. 'I'm happy to see the turnout; it's the biggest I've ever seen.' We were not in Berkeley, or Haight-Ashbury, or some enclave of the liberal West Coast, but in Orange County, formerly one of the most Republican places in America. (Ronald Reagan's political career started here – he once said it was 'where Republicans went to die'.) Jhunjhnuwala had been a Republican herself, but not anymore.

'I voted all Democrats, because I'm mad at the Republican Party. I got mad when Trump got elected. You have to be uneducated and ignorant to vote for the Republican Party right now. Educated women such as myself will think it through cogently and vote accordingly. I had a friend who was hardcore Dem – we used to butt heads. Now we're in total agreement. I can't even believe it myself sometimes.'

The Democratic vote total for the house hit more than 60 million. It was the largest midterms turnout since the beginning of universal suffrage, and the seat pick-up by the Democrats was the largest since the elections after the Watergate scandal. There were seven Orange County seats being contested. Republicans lost every single one.

So was it a 'blue wave'? American punditry obsessed over this question, beginning their speculation before voting had concluded. What happened hadn't even stopped happening, but when the partisan borders on the sectarian, talking points will not be altered by mere events. The most hackish took a leaf from the classic *When Prophecy Fails*, burying their false predictions under a tide of renewed speculation about how the Democrats would govern, or who they would select as their candidates for 2020. Republicans tried to persuade themselves, live on air, that losing the house was actually good news. Their wins in the Senate were unprecedented, and President Trump had personally anointed the victors.

They had their work cut out for them selling this result – the Democrats increased their share of the popular vote by more than eight points, the largest gain since 1948. It was hard for the left to feel disappointed, but there were some shortfalls on the high expectations. Polling had favoured progressive 'superstar' candidates in Southern races – the Florida and Georgia gubernatorial elections, and a Texas Senate spot – but either shy Trump voters or extra-motivated rural, white and older voters blunted these insurgencies. Six months ago, a Democratic challenger receiving 48 per cent of the vote against Ted Cruz in Texas was improbable and would have been considered an excellent result (the state has not elected a Democrat to the Senate since 1988). Instead it was rued as a near miss.

'High voter turnout favours Democrats' is a vintage cliché of American politics. It already looked hoary, and in this wash-up will be retired. Young voters and voters of colour arrived en masse, but so did white rural voters who favour the president and his style. As Dave Weigel noted, the Democratic candidate for governor in Ohio, Richard Cordray, won more votes than the moderate John Kasich did four years ago. Kasich won in a two-to-one landslide, but yesterday 'Trump-era Ohio Republicans

simply smashed through the model with rural voters', seeing
Republican Mike DeWine win. American rancour is written up
as bitter division, but is as often enthusiastic combat.

As with the rise of President Trump, these midterms can't be
separated from a forty-year realignment of white working-class
men away from labour parties and towards conservative parties.
Two decades ago, white working-class men and college-educated
women voted roughly the same way. Now their behaviour at
the ballot box is separated by a 75-point gap. In the 'purple'
suburbs in states like Illinois and California, Republicans shed
college-educated female voters, and lost long-time red seats in
the process. In Orange County, the Putinphilic congressman
Dana Rohrabacher was ousted after fifteen terms.

Internationally, conservatives are more prone to complain
about a 'democratic deficit', especially when dealing with multi-
lateral institutions such as the European Union. In the United
States, the deficit favours the Republicans. The US electoral system was formulated with anti-majoritarian measures in mind,
and as the country becomes more liberal, coastal and diverse, a
regional premium ratchets up the power of white, rural voters
dramatically. In theory, the percentage of the national population required to elect a Senate majority is only 17 per cent. This
time around, some liberals complained about the discrepancy in
the seats won and the 'Senate popular vote'. Democrats had 'won'
by twelve points, but lost multiple seats. In reality, this reflected
an unfavourable map: Democrats were defending twenty-six
states, and Republicans just nine, and many of those Democratic seats were in Trump-friendly states like North Dakota
and Missouri. They did well to hold West Virginia and Mon-
tana, under the circumstances. Voter suppression and district

gerrymandering added to this structural disadvantage.

Just hours after the result, Trump fired his constantly humiliated attorney-general, Jeff Sessions, and replaced him with a deputy more amenable to soft-pedalling the Mueller investigation. The man overseeing it, Rod Rosenstein, was also removed. Last year, South Carolina senator Lindsey Graham said there would be 'holy hell to pay' if Trump fired Sessions. Instead, he tweeted: 'I look forward to working with President @realDonaldTrump to find a confirmable, worthy successor so that we can start a new chapter at the Department of Justice and deal with both the opportunities and challenges our nation faces.'

'The midterm elections used to be, like, boring,' Trump told a crowd in Cleveland, immediately before polls opened. 'Now it's, like, the hottest thing.' The same was true of its consequences.

ROBERT DOESN'T LIVE HERE ANYMORE

I have a mildly confessional face, which means strangers feel compelled to tell me things. My natural mode of small talk is inquisitive, like the good cop in an interrogation, and I attract oddballs, although not as many as I used to. Together, these factors together mean the occasional reception of terrible secrets. Once, a man I asked for directions confessed to an unprosecuted murder (in fact, a double murder); a woman blurted out a cancer diagnosis nobody else knew. A confessional face can be useful for a writer, although its consequences are sometimes unwelcome.

I mention this only because it means I can recognise a related quality, a much rarer one, which is the ability not just to encounter this strangeness and revelation, but to manifest it. It is roughly the difference between being a weirdo magnet and being Weirdo Magneto. So it is not blurbspeak to call Patricia Lockwood a writer of 'rare power': she has a confessional face, and also a self-confessional face, and emanates a humorous and apparently limitless energy that blends and blurs the reality around her. She attracts eccentrics the way hunting deities are depicted attracting beasts, and her chosen habitat of Savannah, Georgia, is teeming with them.

She moved to Savannah almost on sight, because it is so beautiful and so strange, and a reader encountering her work for the first time could trip over this geography, mistaking her poetry as Southern Gothic played for laughs, everything made supernaturally lush and fervent by marsh air. But she was born in the Midwest – living in 'all the worst cities of the Midwest', Cincinnati, Ohio, and Fort Wayne, Indiana – and they honed her style like whetstones. She is also part of that first generation of writers to be shaped by the internet, from a time when it was still called the information superhighway. I suppose it's odd, to think about Weird Twitter and Something Awful being influential the way that *Encounter* or *The Criterion* once were. But without that lineage – first coders, then jokers, then journalists who picked up what she calls the 'crisp new style', recognisable immediately – the elements in her work that might be termed 'insanely online' will be missed.

On the way to Savannah, driving from the mystery of St Helena Island in South Carolina, I listened to Lockwood read the audio version of her newest book. It is an autobiographical work (although it is really not so readily classifiable as this) called *Priestdaddy*. As the semi-official poet laureate of Twitter, she is best known for both poetry and brevity, so it was interesting to hear her for a longer spell, keeping me company in the distance between Cracker Barrel family restaurants. Length can seep the wit out of comic memoir, like a dinner guest who tells one anecdote too many, but *Priestdaddy* holds that sustain. Its imagery is so crowded, so populated with what Lockwood calls her 'private zoo of description', that together it becomes a kind of hyper-analogy for her life, and everyone else's. She also records the early advent of being online lovingly, like a relative camcording the internet at its birth, before it grew into a brute. It helped birth her voice in return, intense and lewd and personal, the sound of someone ripping off the tastefulness that afflicts American letters, performing the literary equivalent of that tablecloth magic trick.

Though we had never met, listening to the book created the uncanny sensation I had already spoken to Patricia Lockwood for ten hours and sixteen minutes, so it felt perfectly natural when she did not offer much in the way of hellos. It just ... *began*.

Her chosen meeting place was Lafayette Square, near the Cathedral of St. John the Baptist, and at first I thought the holy ground had decided the location. Much of *Priestdaddy* is about Catholicism – Lockwood's father found God while watching *The Exorcist* on a nuclear submarine, the *USS Flying Fish*. He viewed it seventy-two times that patrol, and by the end he had a calling: first a dalliance with Lutheranism, and next stop Rome, with his family in tow. For Lockwood, this is an unordinary enough lineage to feel like destiny. Like being the seventh son of a seventh son, 'daughter of a Catholic priest' (especially a possibly psychopathic, guitar-shredding Catholic priest who often wears nothing but underpants) is itself a claim to uniqueness, poet or not. ('What exactly do Catholics believe? ... First of all, blood. BLOOD,' she writes.) But that is not why we were there at all.

'We are here ... on the off-chance of seeing a large tortoise called *Robert*,' she said, 'and he is often in this park.' That explained the diffident eye contact – it wasn't shyness; she was scanning the lawns for this creature.

Robert, Patricia explained, would perambulate here, eating leaves, being petted, having his photo taken. She had a photo already, on her phone. The reptile looked very large, but he was still a juvenile, and would outlive his owner by decades. When anyone asked about this, the man would only say darkly that 'arrangements had been made'.

'Sometimes, Robert is at the bar with his owner,' said Patricia, her tone implying that we would be going to that bar soon. First, though, we would wait in the park, surrounded by oaks old enough to shade it, until we got bored or hungry. Already, two minutes in, we were not having an interview anymore. We were on a tortoise stake-out.

In the meantime, Lafayette Square transformed into a menagerie of other animals. It was the kind of clumsy analogy – an actual private zoo of descriptions – that sounds like bullshit when written down, but I have the photos on my phone. There was a pig in bumblebee wings, then a chihuahua in a little fire-chief costume, and his owner, dressed as a dalmatian. It was the trailing end of an event called Wag-o-ween, and Lockwood cooed and asked questions of the animals and their owners, as though she was there in an official capacity, the Wag-o-ween queen, or its patron saint. She asked their names and breeds, petting and cosseting, offering judicious compliments, taking more photos. 'Oh, I *love* Wag-o-ween,' she said. These sorts of events happened all the time in Savannah. There is a Pirate Day, and something called The Blessing of the Animals, which sounds sacrilegious but is just Franciscan. There was no Robert, though. We were not being blessed.

So instead we talked, somewhat reluctantly, about writing. Many bad descriptions of Patricia Lockwood's physical appearance have been written, partly because this is a legal requirement

of shitty profile journalism, partly because lesser talents are trying to ape her style and partly because she sometimes writes
about sex, so descriptions take on a gross and horny component through interviewer transference. Curiously, none of
these sketches ever mentions her voice. Maybe trapping it on
the page is futile. But it is central to Patricia Lockwood. She
can hit emphases as well as any stand-up. She can mimic, or
declaim. There is a video of her in a Miami bookstore, reading that section from *The Corrections* where Franzen goes on
and on about mixed grills, and she performs it in an accent she
invented, which sounds something like Tallulah Bankhead pre-
senting *The Twilight Zone*. The woman filming it is laughing so
hard there is camera shake. It's mockery, obviously, but it is not
just mockery, and it's not a parody, either. So what is it? That's the
trouble with trying to pin down Lockwood's work with comparisons, because her work is not like anything else, and so people
keep trying to stick precedents to her, and miss the point.

They especially miss the point because of the jokes, the
sometimes-lewd jokes. Lockwood thinks of herself more as a
British ironist than an American one, rescuing all those forbidden
adverbs and exclamation points, and I can see why. 'I think that I
was a very early Anglophile and Canadia-phile. Commonwealth
literature, pretty much. A lot of times that is where the locus of
humor is – just in the dialogue tag, plus adverb. And then you
have Stephen King criticising J.K. Rowling or whatever for using
too many adverbs. But that's the British humorist tradition.'

There is something of that tradition in her obsession with
animalia, too. This kind of thing is not always welcome in
America, or anywhere – the *Private Eye* satirist Craig Brown
once said that Peter Cook would have been considered the equal

of Harold Pinter or Samuel Beckett, had he been less funny. But so far Lockwood is proving the adage that the opposite of funny is not serious; the opposite of funny is not funny.

It helps that she is occasionally, and quietly (there are two tribute adverbs), such a good literary critic herself. She learned a lot of technique from critical essays, because when she was poor she could read them for free on the internet (this, she says, 'is an interesting thing about me'). Sometimes she would read essays about a book before she read the book, developing a taste or interest that is very impressionistic. 'I really feel my way through it, because people write with their bodies. They write the people that they are, and I think there's a gap in criticism, which has been dominated by, you know, old white dudes for so long.' A gap through which a less reactive reading can enter.

Here is Lockwood writing about Joan Didion for the *London Review of Books:*

> 'I have figured out her rhythm,' I once told a friend in a diner in Iowa City, though I will not tell you what I ate, or what I was wearing. (A hamburger? Some sort of shirt?) 'Her sentences are smooth, are smooth, are smooth, and then three-quarters of the way through the landing gear drops down.'

This is a triple parody of Didion. The scene is Didion-like, while also leaving out the Didion detail of the outfit, in an essay about Didion leaving things out. Both the 'are smooth, are smooth, are smooth' sentence and the whole little paragraph are themselves written in the 'landing gear' style. It has the fractal sophistication common only to the finest writing, where the part mimics the whole at every ratio of scale. It also retrieves and presents the fundamental essence of Joan Didion's writing, and is funny at the same time. It does it all in three sentences.

Someone once pointed out that in his fiction, Martin Amis often takes the worst possible premises ('What if poets and screenwriters swapped?') and then makes the best possible stories out of them. That's what Lockwood does, but for whole genres. I defy you to think of a genre with worse potential than 'comedy erotica'. It is uncalled for, has no obvious audience, invites mockery, is inches away from the dirty joke and is also – and this is criminally under-recognised – a nightmare to write from a technical point of view. Good writers wind up as finalists in the Bad Sex in Fiction Award every year, but Lockwood is a better writer, who can somehow seize this nonsense and control it, on Twitter, to both critical and popular audiences, on purpose.

'You would think at some point that people would get the idea that these aren't actually sexy, but they never, never do,' she once told *Hazlitt,* referring to her 'sext' tweets, and those people keep creating a tension between this form and her upbringing and the rest of her style, and it is a tension that doesn't exist. It's like the way living things interact in the film *Annihilation,* only for metaphors. Her mind jumps, her thoughts are flitting, she is always observing, commentating, diverting, but then she presents something whole, no matter how surreal. She can also do it live – it was not until afterwards, reading my transcripts, that I clocked the effect in this exchange:

> RC: There's obviously some religious element to your poetry, and I was wondering if it was liturgical or sacramental, if that makes sense?

PL: It does make sense – but it's obviously both. If you are gunning for a revelation at the end you have to go through the liturgy first, right? You have to engage in the ritual and that's when the ecstatic experience or the revelation comes. That's when the clouds open – that's the idea – so you have to have one in order to have the other.

RC: That's very Catholic.

PL: I know, right?

RC: That's the hocus pocus.

PL: We love the hocus pocus. I'm so hungry.

RC: Let's eat.

PL: I really need to eat, yeah.

The line taken from liturgy to sacrament to comestibles – is it a diversion at all, from someone who grew up eating unconsecrated wafers like crackers?

All of a sudden we were inside Flannery O'Connor's childhood home. It was right by the square, and before we knew it, we were on a tour, being led through antique rooms by a bright-faced volunteer with a mid-Atlantic accent. The sign out the front advertised the former O'Connor residence in iron letters: 'She grew up in this house, and in later years, referred to it simply as "the house I was raised in"'. Fair enough.

The house's parlour, built before air-conditioning, had the look of a room always in shade, with small old furniture, all sub-clinically depressed and evoking childhood mortality. There was also a sponsored library named after Jerry Bruckheimer, the Hollywood director and producer, and all the tour-goers expressed surprise that he was a Flannery fan. Inside, there was a magnet for sale featuring an O'Connor quote: 'There's many a bestseller that could have been prevented by a good teacher,' and an old children's book called *The Fairy Babies,* in which a young O'Connor had written 'Not a very good book' in pencil.

In the kitchen, tin utensils were laid out on the table, as though ready for surgery rather than cooking. The light had a tint to it. 'You can see there the stained glass with a peacock,' the guide said. 'Flannery loved peacocks – they were something of a symbol for her – although she believed that the word "peacock" was vulgar, and called them "peafowls" instead.'

'Peafowls,' Patricia said, with so much pleasure she went agog.

Upstairs: Flannery's childhood bedroom, full of sanctified bric-à-brac, and her parents' room, with a négligée hanging on the wall (it may have belonged to Flannery's mother). Lockwood rolled this object over her mind, calling it a 'negli-jayyyyy'. Under the windowsill was a white wooden frame on wheels, about the size of a chest of drawers, with mesh along on the top and sides. Calling it a 'crib' would be a euphemism – it is a patented product called a Kiddie-Koop, which is really a baby cage. The room was almost too perfect a Freudian diorama for O'Connor: trapped in the baby cage, staring at the négligée. Someone had printed out the old catalogue ad for the Koop, and Patricia read from it in an old-timey voice: 'An over-handled baby is sickly. An indoors baby is pale and listless. And fretful is the tot whose mother unnecessarily worries.' She was practically ecstatic.

There is some long, indistinct line between Flannery O'Connor and Patricia Lockwood. They're both Savannah writers. They both dwell on blackly comic description in a way that is atypically American, and somehow Catholic instead. When O'Connor writes in 'A Good Man Is Hard to Find' about a woman 'whose face was as broad and innocent as a cabbage and was tied around with a green head-kerchief that had two points on the top like rabbit's ears', that innocent cabbage is Lockwoodian. Their works share a sensation of surprise at the end. Flannery O'Connor did not, though, repeatedly say the word 'peacock' on purpose once finding out it was vulgar, nor was her 'thing' 'chugging a Red Bull' before a reading. Not long ago Patricia had developed an allergy to caffeine – it caused heart palpitations – so this signature move was cancelled, and when we got a coffee she was forced to order something boring. 'It's the tragedy,' she says. 'The tragedy of my life.'

The other tragedy of her life is the politics. She has less sympathy for her father's views since *Priestdaddy* was published; she is more dispirited. He used to listen to Bill O'Reilly and Rush Limbaugh simultaneously, and since the election of Trump, has headed 'further down the spectrum in that extremity of view'. (The shared experience of female friends: their fathers saying things that they did not used to.) 'We assume that the arc of the moral universe always bends towards justice, but does it? … What we're experiencing is information sickness. It is warfare against us. We cannot keep up with all these things.' She could not move from bed during the Kavanaugh hearings, and because of the things she has written about, had a constant stream of contact from 'people in similar circumstances'. 'They would say, "I need help. I need help from someone who understands."' It made it seem worth it. 'Poets are against presidents. You have to be, you have to be against world powers.'

There were news stories about someone placing plastic googly eyes on a Savannah historical monument ('Who did this?!' the city asked on Facebook). It was not one of the many municipal statues celebrating the Confederacy, but we planned to look at it anyway, until the plan ran into the bar. The bar was called Pinkie Master's, a rehabilitated dive, meaning they had removed a massive Confederate flag from the wall, and upped the prices, and kept everything else the same. There was still a corner of the flag in a glass case, maybe as a warning. In the 1970s, a boozed Jimmy Carter climbed on a table here to launch his successful presidential run, and in the 2010s, Robert would sit outside with his owner.

The barman seemed pleased to see us, until we asked about the tortoise, and then the smile vanished. 'The owner is not welcome here anymore,' he said. 'He overstepped.' What had happened? Was it a lifetime ban? 'He won't be back.'

The crime was nameless. The profile was now so secondary to the sleuthing it felt like a cover story. But the barman wouldn't talk. We ordered a couple of awful drinks with tequila.

Patricia warmed up by interrogating me. Her style was unique – clownish, manipulative, effective. Somehow the topic turned to her hanging out with Kamila Shamsie. Patricia had been pouring scorn on cricket, and the Pakistani–British novelist had turned out to be a big cricket fan, and something in my face must have changed.

'Oh … You're a cricket fan as well.'

'Well …'

'Exactly why do you like it? Tell me.'

I was about to be made fun of, but the expectancy in her face made me comply. And so I talked about cricket's duration – it was opera, not soap opera – the difference in national styles of play, how it was one of the few sports where players (tail-end batters) were forced to do something they weren't good at; the starring role of the ball, which, unlike in baseball, was tended to then discarded … She asked question after question, and luxuriated in how absurd and boring it all was, and how stupid I was for liking it.

Reeling people in on a line of gentle bullying is also a Lockwood signature. After a while her old schoolfriend Maryann, a librarian, showed up, and got a similar treatment – a series of outrageous questions, provocations and trash talk that she dealt with deftly. This was part of the reason Maryann was so close. 'She once told us,' Maryann said, 'that after we were all dead, she would be remembered for her writing, and if we were remembered at all, it would be as characters in her life,' and this got another burst of laughter on the retelling. Perhaps it was only because I was primed, but watching Patricia and Maryann reminded me of a spell by a wily spinner, full of disguise and drift and deception, working the umpire, making exaggerated appeals, while a batter played watchful defence with soft hands and a dead bat, and tried not to swing at the wrong one.

'Why don't we all play cricket,' said Patricia. 'You can show me.' The tone was an insult comic inviting an audience member on stage.

We stopped by her apartment to pick up the 'equipment' (tennis balls, a rainbow umbrella and a furry hat she insisted on wearing), but I suspected we were there mainly so she could force me to try a drink called Hint®, water with a hint of pineapple. 'It's amazing,' she said. 'Hint! They have a special method for making it. They somehow force the pineapple into the water.'

It tasted like water left in a cupboard with a pineapple. It should be called Taint. But I didn't want to be rude, guessing that this commitment to a mediocre product was because of the caffeine issue. I drank the damn Hint®.

A white-and-black cat entered the room. 'That's Fenriz,' she said.

'Like the mythological wolf?'

'Like the drummer from Darkthrone.'

I know this could sail very close to a hipsterish affectation in someone else, the way people get into theremin playing and obscure British football clubs and so compose a pick-and-mix personality. But it was real. It came from endless roiling curiosities and compulsions. No dilettante would watch the Scandinavian black-metal documentary *Until the Light Takes Us* twenty-five times in a row during a period of depression. (You will notice that this event echoes the Lockwood paternal conversion story – repeat viewing of satanic cinematic material during a period of artificial exclusion, trapped away from the outside world, in the deep.)

So the cat was responsible for a conversation about extremity in the arts, whether the occult was a good means for understanding the current American government (it was), the hidden element of 'blood magic' in identity politics, whether or not Catholicism was the most metal denomination (this may have been exactly why her guitar-playing father left the Lutherans) and which Darkthrone album was the best (agreement on *A Blaze in the Northern Sky;* she owns a copy on vinyl).

[This also explained why, in her audiobook, she imitates the '*ooo ah ah ah ah*' sound from the Disturbed song 'Down with the Sickness', something I thought I must be imagining when

I heard it while driving across the Georgia state line. 'That is a little Easter egg,' she said. *Deadspin* even wrote an article called 'No One Can Do The "OOH WAH AH AH AH" Part From That Disturbed Song', a grudging celebration of the vocal feat that begins the 'chode-rock anthem'. This is incorrect – Patricia Lockwood can do it.]

She also wanted to show me a clip from a reality show called *Southern Charm: Savannah,* because one of the 'stars' lived locally. The clip showed an ill-fated marriage proposal, and the spectacle of a sunburnt douchebag on a boat, sobbing, off-camera, into a radio mic, was so perfectly awful, and struck such an atonal chord of different emotions, that for a moment this cultural brain-rot fermented into something beautiful and poetic. It was just the kind of pop-culture manure that enriches Patricia's work, and grows strange things.

A tree in the park did for stumps. Her bowling action was the slingy style Americans have because they have never seen anyone doing it before. I bowled a leg break, and she hit it out of the meat of the umbrella. We tried some sledging – after all, she should have been a natural at the 'chat' – but it only felt mean here in Georgia, away from an oval. She was panting, not with exertion but with relish, and whenever a bemused onlooker asked if we were playing cricket, she was quick to say yes.

Drinks were taken at Pinkie Master's, where a Yorkshireman asked if we were the ones who had been playing. He began to tell his life story to Patricia (there was that confessional face) – the merchant navy, homelessness – while I got more drinks. The barman was back to bonhomie, and because of the match, he talked about his time in Australia: the sun, the slang. 'I will tell you my filthiest piece of Aussie slang,' I said, 'if you tell me what happened to Robert.'

He sighed. 'The guy was out the front all the time, you know, drinking way too much, and there were questions about how he was getting home, and getting the tortoise home.' So he was drink driving? 'Not just that. I mean, there were questions about where all those drinks were going. I mean, he was ordering a *lot*.' Wait – you mean *Robert* may have been drunk? 'I dunno, man. But also, it was there in a black plastic container or whatever. Like a fucking coffin. The whole thing was just a fucking travesty, man. It shouldn't be there! It's a wild animal! It just shouldn't be outside a bar in a bin!'

I thanked him. (The slang is unrepeatable.)

Meanwhile, Patricia already had the Yorkshireman's full life story, and his admiration. He paid a compliment to her special-ness so effusive that she smirked at me from under her hat, and I wrote it down in my phone. But that night I drove back to the island with the static of 'In the Shadow of the Horns' blaz-ing the whole way, and in the morning, when I looked for the note, it was gone.

SANTA MUERTE

When Erika Peña dropped something on the floor of his truck, and reached down to pick it up and touched a gun instead, she did not startle. This was Texas – a gun in a truck was hardly unusual – and she knew that he needed it for work. Besides, the man that she called David had treated her well most of the time. There was one flash of anger where he had broken her phone, but otherwise, as she told her mother, he acted 'like a gentleman'. They had been visiting his house together for months, taking the brief drive from Laredo to a newish middle-class development near an expanse of scrubby desert, and in the course of these dates, their relationship had morphed from client and sex worker into something less transactional.

But now, inside the place on Bur Oak Drive, an unfamiliar tension was developing into a full-blown unease, and he sensed it. 'Are you scared of me?' he asked, and though she was alone with him, and isolated in this strange patch of suburbia, Erika Peña felt a surge of bravery, and said the name of her murdered friend: Melissa Ramirez. The moment she did, she knew.

David seemed to disappear, replaced by someone else. The kindness shed itself. His face changed into one she had never seen before: eyes blank, head lolling back – 'like something out of *The Exorcist*', she thought – and when he moved to approach her from behind, she felt a chill pass through her, a sensation of death so proximate that her body revolted from it, and she burst out of the front door and vomited in terror, right there in his front yard.

This became her excuse. She was sick, she needed cigarettes, and so they had to leave. Perhaps David thought of all the law-enforcement officers among his neighbours, or of some memory attached to the house itself (his wife and children had been living there for so long). But for some reason he agreed, and they drove the tense few minutes to the Valero gas station on the loop road close by.

The featureless landscape makes this part of Laredo seem semi-remote at first, but 7000 trucks pass through the city every day, long-hauling from the border. These apparently spare highways are so trafficked with heavy freight – semi-trailers laden with whitegoods, or avocados, or whatever else America needs – that the desert traffic can snarl, and the gas station caters for these trucks with a separate car park, almost out of sight. This was where he pulled in his white Dodge Ram, between two trailers.

They talked. They argued. Erika said Melissa's name again, and he responded by grabbing her shoulder and pressing a pistol into the middle of her chest. The muzzle was touching her breastbone, but he seemed to hesitate for a moment, and through her fear, Erika twisted against his clenched hand. She fought. She reached for the horn, and as he restrained her, something gave way – her shirt – enough for her to shed it and wrangle herself free. Then she was running and screaming, not looking back.

Wearing only her bra, she ran towards the blur of lights, expecting the whole time to hear a shot from behind, but instead in front of her, among the fuel dispensers, was a state trooper in his patrol car. 'He's trying to kill me!' she screamed. And then she was in the vehicle, finally safe. (Later, her mother would fixate on this short distance, wondering exactly how far her daughter had had to run.)

There are a few minutes – only a few – in the life of her assailant that go unaccounted for here. They may have been spent sitting alone in a vehicle, or taking a circuitous route, but soon he was home again. In his living room he arranged a small arsenal of firearms – an AR-15, a shotgun, the same pistol from his truck – and waited for the police to arrive, an encounter he was not preparing to survive.

The police were already taking a statement from Erika Peña. The trooper who had rescued her knew the men investigating Melissa Ramirez's murder, and took this possible eyewitness to them immediately. They would not get far on a first name, and Erika was usually not good with directions (her family joked that she didn't know the way to her own house), but she remembered he had a very distinctive job.

'He's a border patrol agent,' she told them.

A short time later, a SWAT team was breaking into his house. He was gone. They found the guns – or most of them, anyway. One, a Heckler & Koch .40 calibre pistol, was not there. This was the same gun Erika had been threatened with, and police were about to discover that it was already a murder weapon twice over. In the next few hours, it would be used to kill two more women.

It was Border Patrol Agent Juan David Ortiz's government-issued service weapon.

★ ★ ★

Laredo, Texas, is one of the twin cities that straddle the US–
Mexico border, and like much of the southernmost United States,
it has a predominantly Hispanic population. By some counts the
city is 96 per cent Hispanic, and it is so close to Mexico that you
can stand on the banks of the Rio Grande and call out to fisher-
men and picnickers on the other side.

Despite this continuity, no one would say that Nuevo Laredo,
Mexico, and Laredo, Texas, are the same place. Laredo is ordinarily a very safe city – much safer than many other urban areas
in the state of Texas. Nuevo Laredo is not a very safe city. At
night, in some Laredo neighbourhoods by the river you can hear
the staccato chatter of automatic gunfire, the acoustic signature
of the cartels. This violence partly explains why Laredo's attitudes
to the border, and those working along it, are so ambivalent.

One aspect of this ambivalence is very personal: most of the
border patrol agents in Laredo are Hispanic: an affiliation sometimes regarded as treasonous by Mexican migrants, by others as
an expression of loyalty. Among those crossing the border daily,
especially labourers, these Latinx agents have a reputation for a
heavy hand, as if they are trying to prove something.

In the borderlands, where work can be patchy or poorly
compensated, jobs with US Customs and Border Protection
are coveted. They are plentiful (the CBP is the largest law-
enforcement agency in United States, and one of the largest in
the world). The jobs are relatively well-paid and well-pensioned,
but have a high attrition rate. They involve some autonomy and
more power, and in a small place like Laredo some agents take
a pride in their jobs that tips over into arrogance. Some hang

their green uniforms in their cars when off-duty, as though flying their colours.

Juan David Ortiz was different. Within the agency, his reputation was as a careerist, and he was good with analysis and computers. He had a master's degree from San Antonio state university and had served in the Iraq War. Afterwards, he had looked to join the police force before changing course. He had not been rejected or found unfit – instead, he struck a deal where his years in the military would count towards a generous pension. He had recently bought a home for his family.

His former best man noticed that he was drinking more than usual, and taking medication. He frequented sex workers, but by itself this was not noteworthy. The women who walked the long sidewalks of San Bernardo Avenue were used to a clientele in uniform. There had been sex workers in Laredo for a long time (across the border, Nuevo Laredo is known for its Boy's Town, a district of legal brothels), but the locals commented on how many more women seemed to be working, especially in the past five years. You could see them after midnight on the streets around the avenue: leaning in the windows of trucks and cars, sitting on the bench at the route-less bus stop, eating at taquerias, walking to the motels where they held shared rooms.

In many places, women who live on the street tend to be runaways or at the fringes of society, already reported missing, or with no one left to miss them (this, along with misogyny, is why repeat murderers so often target sex workers). This was not always true in Laredo, though. San Bernardo Avenue is the central artery of the city, and this meant that many of the workers had repeat encounters with clients, police, neighbours, shopkeepers, familiar faces and even passing family members.

Melissa Ramirez, who worked there, lived with her mother, Cristina Benavides, in a fenced lot holding a handful of demounted caravans. And so on 3 September, when Ramirez stopped answering her phone, Benavides missed her almost immediately. She went to San Bernardo to look for her daughter and did not find her, but instead saw a friend of Melissa's, a woman named Claudine Luera. Claudine told Cristina that she had not seen Melissa.

Beyond the gas stations and diners and fenced-in hotels of San Bernardo Avenue, out to the north-west of Laredo, there are lightless patches of desert and untravelled roads that almost look abandoned. But this is not an easy place to distinguish between the seen and the unseen, and it is exactly these apparently lifeless lands that are most heavily surveilled, where the electronic eyes of law enforcement and Border Patrol seek smugglers and contraband. The secret places in Laredo are semi-peopled, because they are scrutinised less closely. The truck in the middle of nowhere is the one being watched; the vehicle driving down a dirt track en route to some residential ranchettes is being ignored. And it was here, in one of these blind spots, near some copses of prickly pear, that the body of Melissa Ramirez was found, unconcealed and prone by the side of an access road. She had been shot in the back of the head and neck at close range.

Standing vigil over the body in the morning light, the rancher who found her – he had called 911 – saw the approaching car of a Laredo police officer. It seemed unusually responsive because the officer was not responding to a call at all. His appearance was

happenstance – he was there to look at a property for sale – and
perhaps what happened next came from that unexpectedness, or
the fact that his young daughter was riding in the car with him.
But when the rancher flagged the policeman down – and there
was no way that the driver could not see why, it was unmissable –
the car turned and drove away in an arc of dust.

This shirked duty not only cost time, but also gave investigators a false lead: it was the act of a coward, but looked
indistinguishable from a perpetrator returning to a crime scene,
and then fleeing when discovered.

There was another misleading detail. Melissa Ramirez's
mother had recalled her daughter getting into a black truck,
driven by an older man she had been seeing. This man was identified from Ramirez's phone records, questioned and released
once his alibi checked out. But the black truck somehow became
stuck in the investigators' consciousness, a dead-end description
that swirled among the leads and rumours, until both police and
the women on San Bernardo Avenue were on the lookout for the
wrong man in the wrong vehicle. It became folk knowledge on
the street – 'don't go with a man in a black truck' – and created
a dangerous sense of false security.

Cristina Benavides also remembered that in the weeks before
her daughter's death, Melissa had had a premonition. 'They're
going to kill me, Mom,' she said, 'and they're going to do it like
this,' and with her fingers, she pressed the shape of a gun to her
temple.

She was not the only victim to have had a sense of foreboding.

Claudine Luera was born in the south of Laredo to a Mexican father and a Scottish mother. They had eloped, and after her mother spent her first summer in the Texan city, sweating under the roof of the meagre house they could afford, she turned to her husband and said, 'You've taken me to hell.'

Claudine's sister, Angie Luera-Perez, has her mother's red hair. It had taken her months to speak out about what had happened to her sister, but by December she was trying to retrieve meaning from the tragedy of her sister's death by doing charity work for the homeless, and her living room was filled with donated blankets and care packages.

Angie had felt raw animal grief before this new sense of acceptance. She went without sleep for extended periods, and snapped at her children and co-workers. They had understood. One unbearable evening, she had drifted into half-consciousness and felt the presence of ethereal hands all over her, urging her to finally rest. It was the beginning of a tentative peace, and in trying to maintain it, she aimed to learn as little about Juan David Ortiz as possible.

Angie had had a tough upbringing, but something else had happened to Claudine when she was five. She would never speak about it, but it seemed to strip a vital quality from her for good. 'You don't understand, you're the strong one,' Claudine would say, when her sister remonstrated about her drug use over the phone. It was hard for Angie to watch – the jailbird boyfriends, the long sleeves and glassy distance at Christmas time, protective services removing Claudine's five children. Rehab did not seem to stick.

Claudine kept talking about getting clean for her kids, and her role on the street was semi-maternal. At forty-two, she was older than most of the other girls, but retained a softness at odds with the harshness of her life. Most mornings she would go to the Kwik Chek convenience store on San Bernardo Avenue and order a large strawberry and banana slushie. Abbie Pardo, one of the clerks, remembered how kind she was, how she would always take a moment to ask after her. She remembered, too, how close Claudine and Melissa were.

Claudine's family believe she may have got into Ortiz's truck in an attempt to find out what had happened to her friend, and according to Ortiz's own confession, on the twenty miles of road between the town centre and a mile marker north of Laredo, Claudine began asking questions. There was a confrontation over Melissa, and at a spot among the long grass, now marked by ribbons and a weather-blanched shrine, he ordered her out of the truck.

It was a truck driver who found her, shortly before dawn. She had been shot multiple times in the head at close range, with the same large-calibre handgun. Victims almost never survive assaults of this ferocity, but Claudine did. She managed to crawl in the dark to a place on the verge of the road, where she was visible, and when the driver stepped down from his cab, he found her still breathing. She had been there for nearly five hours.

Among the surprised ambulance crew who rushed to Claudine's aid was someone who knew who she was, the son of one of Angie's co-workers. It was his first time on a traumatic response call, and as they raced the distance to hospital, Claudine began murmuring. So far, this first responder has been too distraught to convey what she said, even to Claudine's immediate family, but Angie took comfort in this coincidence. Later, at her workplace, she encountered a statue of Mother Teresa and wept.

She had learned that the saint offers succour 'for the people who were thrown by the side of the street'.

One of the nurses assigned to Claudine's hospital room was an acquaintance as well, and when the mortally wounded woman's condition became irretrievable, she laid on her hands. Once Claudine Luera finally succumbed to the massive damage the bullets had done to her person, the nurse coded her. It was afternoon. A few hours later, Juan David Ortiz was picking up Erika Peña.

From the moment he killed Melissa Ramirez, Ortiz must have expected to be caught. Now it was inevitable. He was no longer a murderer; he was a spree killer. He knew Melissa Ramirez and Claudine Luera personally. He had used a weapon that could be traced, and left shell casings at the scene of both shootings.

Once Erika Peña escaped, it was over. She could recognise him by sight. His truck was identifiable on the gas-station surveillance cameras. Ortiz did not intend to be captured alive, and weighing up what he believed would be the final moments of his life, he left behind his cache of twelve guns, all fully loaded, taking only the freshly fired handgun. Around this time he posted two messages to Facebook: 'To my wife and kids, I love u' and 'Doc Ortiz checks out. Farewell' (Doc was his nickname from the Navy). Then he got back into his Dodge Ram and made the return trip through the night, towards Laredo's centre.

With her daughter still being questioned by police, Erika Peña's mother, Adriana Rodriguez, was unaware of the attempted kidnapping. Around 11.30pm, she was lying in bed, smoking, when she heard a sound: someone was trying to open her front door. The would-be intruder couldn't breach it, and by the time Rodriguez ran to the window, she could make out only the departing shape of a white truck.

Word of Claudine Luera's death had reached San Bernardo Avenue, and while the women knew they would be targets, they kept working. Whether the news had reached Griselda Cantu is unknown. Griselda, who most people knew as Chelly, was trying to work. A lonely, isolated figure on the streets, she was quiet and seldom in trouble. She carried her possessions in a backpack, and would sometimes sit, packing and repacking it. Her unhappy life seems to have left few traces.

In the early minutes of 14 September 2018, at around 12.07 pm, authorities released a 'be on the lookout' (BOLO) notice that identified Juan David Ortiz, and included a description matching his truck. Griselda was picked up at almost exactly the same time, around midnight. When the notice became public knowledge, Griselda was already inside the vehicle. Meeting Juan David Ortiz would be her final misfortune.

Together, murderer and victim drove twenty miles north on the Interstate 35, past the fast-food chains and the town's water tower, the gas stations and the flyovers, until the surrounds darkened. This time Ortiz ventured less out of the way, to an overpass on the main highway, with a busy truck stop nearby. The location seemed hastily chosen, bordering on a public place, not free from occasional traffic even after midnight. Police were now patrolling these roads as well, and they knew what Ortiz's empty house meant.

But no police or good Samaritans passed, and no one would discover Griselda until the next day. Like Claudine, she had been shot in the head more than once, and survived. But Griselda would not have had hours of uncertainty. She was bludgeoned with a heavy object after she was shot, and this blunt-force trauma caused her death.

The truck turned around, taking the same course back to San Bernardo Avenue. Judging by how far he travelled, Ortiz must have been driving fast.

Janelle Enriquez had been defending herself from a young age. When she was nine years old, her father, Armando Ortiz, taught her a move called *la metralleta* – 'the machinegun', a flurry of quick punches. The first time she employed it, a school bully hit the ground face-first, 'like an ostrich'. Armando hadn't been happy when Janelle transitioned; he still sometimes slipped and called her his 'son'. His trepidation, it turned out, did not come from bigotry. It came from fear – the fear of how hard and dangerous life could be for a woman.

Janelle Enriquez 'could throw hands', her cousin Lorena Gomez remembered, and she had cause to: violence and death were part of her life. Janelle's grandfather and great-uncle had both been murdered years before; another great-uncle, drunk and depressed, had walked into the waters of the Rio Grande; a long-term lover had been jailed for a killing. When Janelle prayed to a saint, she would make votives to Santa Muerte, the saint of death. This deity takes the form of a Grim Reaper in feminine robes, and her millions of worshippers are found across Central America and the Mexican diaspora in the United States, where she is patron to the marginalised and imperilled.

Criminals, beggars, sex workers and the LGBTQIA community seek her aid, which is said to be offered without judgement. Janelle had a large shoulder tattoo of Santa Muerte, as well as a statuette of the saint. Privately, her family worried about her. Curtailment of her young life, by accident, overdose or disease, was foreseeable. Once, when a woman was murdered in Laredo, Armando feared it was Janelle, and was so distraught his face became paralysed. When Melissa Ramirez was killed, she was wearing a top borrowed from Janelle.

At the end of August, Janelle was watching Aretha Franklin's funeral on television and saw the singer lying in repose, dressed in a red sequinned dress. 'That's how I want to go,' she said to her aunt. And that was how she went, resplendent, with a red flower behind her ear, her made-up face still swollen from the wound that ended her life. Her body had been identified by her shoulder tattoo.

Her sister Rosenda could not stop remembering a troubling detail: days before, the head of Janelle's Santa Muerte statue had broken off. 'This means something bad will happen to me,' Janelle said. Rosenda kept looking up what it meant.

'My sister didn't have a picture of the serial killer look,' Rosenda said. Sometimes she blamed the statue. Perhaps Janelle thought fate or fists would protect her; she was aware enough to warn others on the strip. That night she was working with a friend, Stephany Gonzalez, and the two joked as they strolled outside lightless residences. The truck driver who approached them was jumpy and seemed ready to drive away when a car came near. But nervous, shamed clientele were not so unusual on San Bernardo Avenue, and Janelle could handle herself. Stephany had a bad feeling and gripped a pocketknife under her shirt. Janelle got into the truck.

Months later, Armando would follow the same route as his daughter, down the I-35, and as the car began to pick up speed on that blank stretch of highway, he became silent. 'It's a long way,' he said finally. The destination was a weedy, marker-less place where the road ran parallel to railroad tracks. It was unremarkable – even the high piles of gravel that distinguished it had been removed – and Armando wandered through the thicket as though making sure this was definitely the place it happened. Like Claudine Luera and Erika Peña, Janelle Enriquez confronted Juan David Ortiz. Her family believe she showed courage, defiance. According to Ortiz's confession, her last words were something like, 'If you're going to do it, then do it.'

On the morning of 16 September, around 1.00 am, two Texas Highway Patrol Troopers drove past the Valero gas station on San Bernardo and Jefferson Street, and saw the unmissable frame of a white Dodge Ram truck in the parking lot, empty and unat-tended. With no sign of the driver, they could come close enough to see through the window. Inside, unhidden, was a Heckler & Koch P-2000 .40 calibre pistol. They knew whom it belonged to. Ortiz had gone in unarmed, to use the restroom, and so the troopers drew their tasers and approached the storefront.

Their quarry, out of the bathroom and into the store, saw them trying to enter and ran out a side entrance before they could fire. Juan David Ortiz sprinted down San Bernardo Avenue. Half a block further on his left was a wide, steep con-crete ramp rising to a parking lot: the rear of the Hotel Ava. He hid himself among the cars.

Often, when there is a police incident in Laredo, the first civilian on the scene is a woman named Priscilla Trevino. She is better known as Lagordiloca – 'the crazy fat lady' – and has more than 100,000 followers on Facebook, an audience that takes in half the city. Her livestreams break news often ('she has a mouth bigger than a church door,' one border patrol agent said), and sure enough, as a SWAT team prepared to storm the Hotel Ava, there she was filming and broadcasting with her phone.

Some of those watching the stream headed down to take a look. And that was how Janelle Enriquez's family came to be present, watching on San Bernardo Avenue as Juan David Ortiz was arrested. They did not yet know that Janelle was dead, or that Ortiz had killed her.

Inside the parking lot, the fugitive had pointed his phone at the officers like a gun, hoping to be shot. His 'suicide-by-cop' attempt failed. He was taken to a sheriff's substation nearby and, not long afterwards, asked if his handcuffs could be removed. His videotaped confession was meticulous. It lasted more than nine hours, and all that time Ortiz expressed no remorse. He delivered his report like an analyst, programmatically. Just after the ninth hour, he admitted to the killing of Janelle Enriquez, though he knew her only by a slur, and two officers left immediately. Another trip down the I-35.

His attitude was a surprise. He had intended to clean up the streets, or a single street: San Bernardo Avenue. He had expressed 'a hatred of prostitutes'. He had deemed these women unworthy of life.

In Laredo, afterwards, people would try to make sense of these events with the aid of rumour. There was a story, published in a Mexican newspaper and widely believed, that Juan David

Ortiz had contracted a sexually transmitted infection, possibly HIV, from someone he had met on the street. The killings were supposed to be his revenge. It explained why his wife had left, and why he had started to drink.

But Ortiz was, as District Attorney Isidro Alaniz confirmed, 'as healthy as you or me'. Condoms were found in his truck, and police believe that when he committed his crimes, he was sober. Sociopathy and misogyny in combination have led many men to kill before; why they made Juan David Ortiz kill so abruptly, and so often, cannot be determined. Criminologists say the pattern of his offending is almost unheard of. The person who knows him best, his wife, has so far refused to cooperate with authorities. She has visited him in jail, a loyalty that is hard to understand.

When the Webb County District Attorney's office presented its case to a grand jury, the motive was familiar from other mass murderers. Hatred of prostitutes. Cleaning up the streets. The language of the charges was familiar as well – Webb County was seeking the death penalty, and it sought retribution for the 'cold, callous and calculated way' Ortiz had taken life.

The families, some of whom wanted him jailed forever instead, were most upset by something else: the victims, all the victims, Alaniz said during the press conference, knew where they were going. This information, and the dread that it conjured, was the focus of one of the only questions the family asked. Armando was too upset to go inside, and kept pacing outside the courtroom. Claudine Luera's family were wearing T-shirts with a quote from an ee cummings poem: *i carry your heart with me (i carry it in. my heart.)*. Cristina Benevides could not talk about it anymore. Unable to face proceedings, Erika Peña stayed home. No representative of Griselda Cantu made themselves known.

'This case is going cold,' Erika Peña's mother had said, days before the hearing. 'That's what people are saying, but it's not going cold.' It was a strange thing to say about a case with a confession, and what she meant was that the city was already forgetting. Nationally, the crimes seemed to merge with a mass of confusion about the border. Some of the people in the district attorney's office did not even know Ortiz's name, and, when asked about the arraignment, mistook him for another killer border patrol agent, a man who had murdered his lover and a one-year-old boy believed to be their child. None of the families had been contacted by US Customs and Border Protection. Janelle's sister Rosenda blamed the government, and she blamed Laredo. She was coming to hate the city, she said. Her father, Armando, had a dream in which he spilled a cornucopia onto the ground. In a house where Claudine Luera used to stay, one of her former housemates ate his meals with a newspaper photo of her face set across the table from him.

There was someone else. Anna Karen, who grew up with her mother teaching her to steal mail, who grew up sleeping on other people's couches. She had a glass eye, a heroin addiction and loyal-enough clients that one day, she said, a group of five other women jumped her and beat her out of jealousy. For a time, she said, Juan David Ortiz was a client (her neighbour confirmed this contact).

He was obsessed with Erika Peña, Anna Karen said, and 'David' even paid her to try to find Erika, although she couldn't do it on demand.

They would sit in his truck and smoke and he would ask her questions: does Erika use needles? Does she take showers? Does she have Hep C?

'I'd prefer to talk about me,' she said, so they did.

On their last meeting, Ortiz said he wanted to forget about Erika. 'She's the only one who's been to my house, but you can go there too,' he said. 'You can be the second one, you can be the second one to live in my house and make a life with me.'

They went to the drive-thru first, bought some beers. 'Why don't we go to the checkpoint as well,' he said. Anna Karen objected. 'I was like, "No no no, I wanna go home,"' she said. 'And he said, "Okay. I will take you back." On our way back, I was talking about my daughters, my kids. All the conversations I had with him was about my kids, my kids, my kids, nothing else.'

At one point, she had dropped her phone under the seat and got down to look for it. 'I have my gun there,' Juan David Ortiz said.

'Oh, don't take it, don't take it out,' said Anna Karen, who had had a gun pointed at her head before.

'Don't worry about it,' he said. 'I'll just leave it there.'

He gave her some money to try to get clean. He texted her afterwards: *I hope you change later on. You make me proud. You'll change.*

The next time Anna Karen saw him, she said, Claudine Luera was getting into his truck. She thought, 'Claudine is going with my friend.' She had texted him that same day, by mistake. It was a message intended for someone else that read *U2*. He had replied: *Bye.*

ACKNOWLEDGEMENTS

My wife and my family, Han Jianping and Shen Hangmei, Morry Schwartz, Nick Feik, Chris Feik, Julia Carlomagno, Kate Greenwood, Natalie Book, Jessica Reed, Jamie Hall, Dr Dougal Phillips, the old Lacey studio crew, Matthew Thompson, Mikhaela Rodwell, Rob Steinbaum, Rick Perlstein, Anna Clark, Terry Collison, Pastor Steven Little, Jim and Lois Whiteman, Paul Liu and Lemon Fang, Deborah Dicks Maxwell, Patricia Lockwood, Lorena Rios, the Peña/Rodriguez, Ortiz/Enriquez and Luera/Perez families of Laredo, Alexandra Christie, Scott Dooley, Rachel Dry, Tom Lutz and The Thread.

Sections of this book appeared on *The Monthly* website between May and December 2018. 'Santa Muerte' first appeared in *The Guardian*, March 2019.

Printed in the USA
CPSIA information can be obtained
at www.ICGtesting.com
LVHW051037191123
764349LV00008B/482